RHYMING HISTORY

The Story of England in Verse

RHYMING HISTORY
The Story of England in Verse

by Colin Wakefield

Illustrations by John Partridge

VOLUME FOUR: 1649 – 1660

Cromwell and the Commonwealth

DHP
Double Honours Publications

RHYMING HISTORY
The Story of England in Verse

VOLUME FOUR: 1649 – 1660
Cromwell and the Commonwealth

First published in 2014 by Double Honours Publications.

ISBN 978-0-9570120-3-5

Double Honours Publications

Email: info@rhyminghistory.co.uk
Website: www.rhyminghistory.co.uk
Twitter: @Rhyming_History

Printed and bound by Short Run Press, Exeter

AUTHOR'S NOTE

This is Volume Four of our *Rhyming History* (still in the writing), which will eventually stretch from Julius Caesar's invasion of Britain in 55BC to the present day.

Volume Five (Charles the Second and the Restoration) will also be published in 2014, with subsequent volumes appearing annually. All published volumes are available for sale through the website and selected retailers.

These books of verse are intended for those who want to learn about our history, but in not too solemn a way. I hope they will also appeal to a wider audience, students and historians, and those who simply enjoy reading verse.

John Partridge has again provided witty and entertaining illustrations to accompany the text, for which I am as ever most grateful.

My special thanks are due to Jonathan Dowie for his detailed preparation of the text and for mastery of the website. I am also most grateful to Chris Moss for his help with the cover, to Anne Reid and Alan Coveney for their advice on the text, and to Michael Callahan and Chris Wakefield for their continued support.

Please visit our website for updates on future volumes of the *History*, and for news of live performances of the verse.

www.rhyminghistory.co.uk

Colin Wakefield – September 2014

CROMWELL AND THE COMMONWEALTH

Regicide   1649

King Charles the First (from the books that I've read)
Was defiant in death. He lost his head,
One swift stroke of the axe, before a crowd
Of anguished spectators, who groaned out loud.
Not for them the accustomed jubilation
Of a public execution. The nation
Stood in sorrow, shock, confusion and despair.
You couldn't find a subject anywhere,
Outside the Levellers (all half barmy),
Fifth Monarchists, and some in the Army,
Who hailed the murder as a deed well done.
The regicide, a crime second to none,
Was justified without recourse to law,
The trial a farce: justice by the back door.

Cromwell rued the King's death. How could this be?
Ever Charles' political enemy,
In battle his principal adversary,
He pursued him to trial with energy.
He signed the death warrant, the third signatory,
Yet, over the body, "cruel necessity!"
Were the words Cromwell uttered. It has to be said,
He considered the dangers of Charles the First dead
As great, if not greater, as Charles the First living.
I'm not saying Cromwell was soft or forgiving,
Yet he tried for a settlement – oh, how he tried!

But his efforts were thwarted, his struggles denied,
By the King's double-dealing. I took Charles' side,
But his cunning and lies, I have to confess,
Quite altered my views. Now I couldn't care less.

North of the border young Charles was proclaimed King,
According to law. The Scots had been sulking.

They'd not been consulted and made no pretence
Of their anger and outrage, taking offence
At their sovereign's vile, unwarranted death.
Much good did it do them. They wasted their breath.
For the new King hadn't a chance. He was weak.
In exile in France, his prospects were bleak.

Europe

The French couldn't wait to be rid of him.
European politics (sink or swim)
Necessitated the taking of sides,
Even with a rabble of regicides.
The French were wrapped up in a war with Spain,
Hard-fought and bitter. They'd little to gain
From harbouring Charles, spitting in the eye
Of the English *régime*, a prime ally.
So they kicked Charles out ('the Second', so-called).
He crawled to the Dutch, who were duly appalled.

They cold-shouldered the King for the same reason.
To their cost, the Stuarts were out of season.

Cromwell and the Commonwealth

Charles and his brothers finally found a friend
In the King of Spain. Their concord was to end,
As these alliances often do, in tears.
After sucking up to the Spanish for years,
Well nigh a decade, when it came to the crunch
Poor Charles reaped scant benefit. Now it's my hunch
None was intended. The Franco-Spanish pact,
When it came, ignored the Stuarts. That's a fact.
Charles was a laughing stock, no shadow of doubt.
Spain's King chewed him up, before spitting him out.

The crowned heads of Europe (hardly a surprise)
Were struck with horror at the late King's demise,
And the manner of it. How safe were their heads?
Did their own fates hang by the thinnest of threads?
How likely were they to be slain in their beds?
Politics were politics. The regicide,
Though abhorred and awful, could not be denied –
Tantamount to political suicide
To ignore. Cromwell came to be much admired
As the years rolled on. His example inspired.

Royalist hopes at home

In England the prospects of a counter-revolt
Were slim. This wasn't entirely Charles Stuart's fault.
The Royalists, having lost the first Civil War,
Chose (in 1648) to come back for more.
They were met with a veritable *tsunami*.
Overwhelmed by Fairfax's New Model Army,
They were soundly defeated and demoralised –
More fatally than many at first realised.
Throughout the 1650s uprisings were few.
To be blunt, the Royalists hadn't a clue.
There was little, it seemed, their leaders could do.

So what was happening at home? Fair question.
The killing of a King took some digestion!

Rhyming History

First and foremost, men asked, who was in control?
Following the King's, were more heads like to roll?
The regicides knew they would have to act fast –
A new settlement was needed, fit to last.
Regrettably this proved strangely elusive.
Within weeks the Levellers turned abusive,
Accusing Oliver Cromwell and his kind
Of a sell-out. The Levellers, unrefined,
Championed the cause of England's liberty
(As they interpreted it) and, as we'll see,
Were a painful thorn in the new *régime*'s side.
Cromwell in turn gave them a pretty rough ride.

That's for later. The main thing to decide,
In the wake of Charles' death, was where power lay.
Strange to say, not far from where it lies today:
With Parliament. Where else? Not with Cromwell,
Nor with the New Model Army, truth to tell.

Cromwell's authority

I'm talking constitutionally here.
Throughout the Interregnum, year on year,
The truth would become abundantly clear:
Cromwell was the Guv'nor. Why shed a tear?
Without his talent and his vision,
His hatred of drift and division,
England would ever be under the yoke
Of Kings and tyrants, no word of a joke.
The Irish, of course, will never agree –
But they've genuine cause, as soon you'll see.

Underpinning Cromwell's authority,
Of course, all decade long was the Army.
This was the uncomfortable reality.
There existed a deep-seated antipathy
Between Army and Parliament, its pedigree

4

Stretching back to the heady days when the late King
Would play one off against the other, indulging
In the time-honoured tactic of 'divide and rule'.

For Oliver Cromwell was nobody's fool.
He struggled to hold the balance for years –
Many predicted it would end in tears –
Between the Rump (the purged Parliament)
And the Army. It was effort well spent.
There were limits, of course. If something had to give,
He would round on the Rump (far too conservative),
Paying due regard to the Army's frustration
At the lamentable pace of change. The nation
Wanted the firmest authority to save it.
Strong leadership was needed. Oliver gave it.

Cromwell was at heart a facilitator –
Radical, yet an arch-conciliator.
He remained a master, to his dying day,
Of the art of the possible. I must say,
For a man renowned for getting his own way
He was skilled in the subtleties of compromise,
And far more pragmatic than many realise.
Unafraid to confront the more radical factions
In the Army, and undaunted by the reactions
Of his own colleagues, he was nevertheless
A fair man and generous – hence his success.

The institutions of government

In the aftermath of Charles' tragic death
The Rump, it appears, hardly paused for breath.
It showed some radical spirit in fact.
Of necessity, its very first act
Was to declare itself, officially –
Sound sense, speaking constitutionally –
The highest authority in the land.
It's easy, I suppose, to understand

Rhyming History

Why the Rump had to do this. There was no room,
After the King's demise, for a vacuum.

Yet it does occur to me (I could be wrong)
That they made it all up as they went along.
In March the monarchy was swept away,
Which begs the question: why the delay?
And not until two months later, in May,
Was the Commonwealth declared. I must say,
As *coups d'état* go this was pretty tame stuff.
And as if this foot-dragging wasn't enough,
The motion to have the Lords abolished
Was opposed (I'm more than faintly astonished)
By Cromwell, no less. A "great inconvenience,"
The Commons called the Lords. At least the Rump saw sense.

A whole mass of monarchical regalia –
The Privy Council, and paraphernalia
Such as the Exchequer and prerogative Courts,
The Admiralty and departments of all sorts –
Were similarly abolished in one fell swoop.
The new *régime*, naturally, had to 'regroup'.
The Rump legislated for a Council of State
(An Executive) and created a clean slate,
Effectively, by setting up (this all took hours)
Hosts of sub-committees with delegated powers.
Dull, but urgent. Cromwell was first to take the chair
Of the Council. Within days he was in despair.

The oath (or 'Engagement') that members were to swear
Was couched in terms confirming the legality
Of the regicide. I mean! The majority –
Twenty-two of its membership of forty-one –
Refused point blank. Most revealing. All said and done,
This was the most obvious indication yet,
The clearest evidence that one could hope to get,
Of the horror, even within the government,
Felt at the King's foul murder. All too apparent,

I'd say, were the dangers at large. Cromwell, for sure,
Was sensible to the dilemma. He foresaw,
In his own instinctive, inimitable way,
The grave risks in forcing the oath. He had his say.
The wording was changed. With the minimum of fuss
All men swore to "be true" (so, quite innocuous)
"To the Commonwealth of England" (who could refuse?)
"Without a King or House of Lords". Much better news.
Most could subscribe to this oath, whatever their views.

The Rump's achievements, however, were few.
One immediate challenge (nothing new)
Was a crisis in the economy,
The worst of the seventeenth century –
A deep recession. This it took in hand
With a series of measures (nothing grand)
Which included a Navigation Act,
A statute enthusiastically backed

Rhyming History

By every interest. This provided
That all imports (so the Rump decided)
Should only be transported in English ships
Or those of the exporter. This got to grips,
At a stroke, with the stranglehold of the Dutch
In foreign trade, which troubled the English so much.

The Rump established a Council of Trade
To address the crisis. Progress was made
In reversing the downturn, creating wealth,
And restoring the nation to better health.
This at least showed that republicanism,
Born as it was of upheaval and schism,
Was no formula, bred of necessity,
For the breakdown of order, and anarchy.
Indeed, the Rump was too conservative for some,
Obsessed with trifling measures till kingdom come.

The Rump did manage the repeal of statutes, true,
Compelling Church attendance. This was welcome, new,
Progressive and significant. All moves, however,
To abolish tithes were shelved, abandoned for ever.
Presbyterianism survived wholly intact
Owing, in short, to a stubborn reluctance to act.
So much then for radical religious reform.
Inertia, over-caution and fear were the norm.
The Rump did modernise the legal process a bit,
Replacing Latin with English. Sadly, that was it.

Ireland

Another immediate danger, more pressing,
Came from Ireland. Particularly distressing
Was the prospect of Ireland as a launching pad,
Backward as the country was, and however sad,
For the first stab at a Stuart restoration.
Charles, alas, had ideas above his station.

Cromwell and the Commonwealth

Egged on by his chief adviser in exile, Hyde,
Who might just as well have urged him to suicide,
Charles had high hopes of his royalist lieutenant,
James Butler, 12th Earl of Ormonde – a Protestant,
And effective champion of the royal cause
In Ireland since 1640. Let's take a pause…

The greater mass of the Irish were Catholics,
We know that. But their politics were an odd mix,
Their tragic history one of disunity,
Division and distrust. No opportunity
For dissent or disruption was ever missed,
Nor for fighting and fisticuffs. You get the gist?
This is far from my own view, I hasten to add.
The Irish to my mind are neither mad nor bad,
But the best on God's earth. Oliver Cromwell, though,
Was convinced they were wicked, that you should know.
So when Ormonde made a pact with the Catholics,
On behalf of Charles, republican politics
(Fears for England's safety) and naked prejudice
(Hatred of the Irish) threatened mayhem. Mark this:
Cromwell and his credulous cohorts had swallowed,
Wholesale, tales of Irish cruelty and wallowed
(There's no better word for it) in hopes of revenge.

Cromwell had just one thing on his mind: to avenge
(Yes, avenge) the awful slaughter of Protestants,
And their torture, by Catholics. Arrant nonsense.
Exaggerated Protestant spin. For no one
Could recall, no one, however hard they spun,
What truly happened in 1641.
Atrocities were committed, I'll be bound,
On both sides. But no firm proof was ever found
Of the kinds of dreadful deeds that were alleged
To have been done by Catholics. Cromwell pledged,
Nonetheless, to avenge all these horrors. He,
No eye-witness, was the lead authority,
Self-appointed, on Irish atrocity!

Rhyming History

Forgive me, I'm getting carried away.
There's no clear evidence, even today,
That these were Cromwell's motives. I will say,
However, that it seems extremely odd
That he, whose every third thought was God,
Should have behaved in Ireland as he did
(No better than a homicidal kid)
Were he not bigoted and prejudiced
Against the Irish people. Yes, racist.
His own words may be quoted to bear this out:
"All the world knows their barbarism." Have no doubt,
Cromwell loathed the Irish, the Catholics at least.
His name to this day is synonymous with 'beast'.

In March he was named as Commander-in-Chief
Of the Irish campaign. Now, it's my belief –
And I say this entirely without malice –
That his appointment was a poisoned chalice.
Cromwell knew it. Reputations had been lost
In Ireland, as many had found to their cost.
The all-important question of supplies
Had not been addressed. It came as no surprise
That funds were scarce. The City of London failed,
When asked, to furnish loans. Common sense prevailed
When the Rump stepped in and deftly passed an Act
To sell Church lands. A close call, and that's a fact.

Discontent in the Army

More serious was the Army's reluctance
To engage. They led Cromwell a merry dance.
Where did this spring from? Subversive influence!

Leading Levellers had long been critical
Of the Commonwealth leadership. Typical,
They complained, of Cromwell and his acolytes
Was the Rump. This wrong they sought to set to rights.

Cromwell and the Commonwealth

The Levellers were pressing for a franchise
Worthy of the people at large. In their eyes
The Rump was too narrowly representative,
Too stuck in the past. This they couldn't forgive.

John Lilburne published a radical pamphlet
Which rubbished the Rump in the strongest terms yet.
Lilburne denounced "this new kind of liberty"
As no liberty at all. The Treasury,
The Courts and England's forces "by Land and Sea"
Were under the arbitrary governance
Of the Council of State. This was some grievance.
What had become, honest John wanted to know,
Of the liberty of which no man, friend or foe,
Was to be deprived, without the lawful say-so
Of his equals, his fellow countrymen, his peers?

To Lilburne today we give three hearty cheers.
The sad truth is, John was ahead of his years.
His tract, *England's New Chains Discovered*, stoked fears
Not only in the breasts of the old Royalists,
But also the new constitutionalists,
Cromwell included. He was heard to fulminate,
"I tell you again" (this to the Council of State)
"You are necessitated to break them". They did.
The Council, to a man, performed as they were bid.
The leading culprits, Lilburne, William Walwyn,
John Overton and others of their brethren
Were despatched to the Tower. Only John Lilburne,
As we'll see a little later, was slow to learn.

What's all this to do with the Army, and Ireland,
I hear you ask? Well, it helps us to understand
What was rumbling away in the Army ranks.
Were they itching to put down the Irish? No thanks!
They too had their grumbles, not least their wage arrears.
This grouse was quite speedily addressed, it appears,

But a hard core of zealous dissidents remained.
The influence of the Levellers, thought to have waned,
Was hard at work in Henry Ireton's regiment,
At Salisbury. The ringleaders' avowed intent
Was to sit tight in England unless and until
Liberty was secure. Cromwell had had his fill.

Cromwell acts

Learning of a second dangerous mutiny
Hatched in another regiment, in Banbury,
Whose instigators planned to march on Salisbury
To meet up with their fellows, Cromwell and Fairfax
Marshalled their troops to head them off. "He who attacks,"
So goes the military maxim, "wins the day."

I made that last bit up. It's true though, anyway.
For Cromwell took the wretched rebels by surprise,
At Burford, in Oxfordshire. What no one denies
Is that Oliver showed mercy. Before first light
He struck. The rebels could barely manage a fight.
Some were slain. The more fortunate were put to flight.
The remainder, however, a good few hundred,
Were herded into the church. Three were shot dead,
The main agitators. Now it has to be said,
To Cromwell's credit, that to execute so few
Was proof of his strength. Their fellows had a fine view,
From the church roof, of the martyrs, now laid to rest
In unmarked graves in the churchyard, three of the best.

A memorial plaque, recently erected –
A tribute, I'm sure, no one ever expected –
Can be seen on the south wall. There's a fine verse play
(Nowadays rarely performed, I'm sorry to say)
Called *A Sleep of Prisoners,* by Christopher Fry,
Inspired by these events. You've not read it? Do try.

There's a fascinating carving on the font, too:
ANTHONY SEDLEY PRISNER. If he only knew
How his name would be remembered, one of the few!
Do visit Burford if you can. I urge you to.

John Lilburne

Cromwell laid the blame for these events squarely
At John Lilburne's door, a little unfairly.
The Levellers were no longer big hitters.
Yet the Rump displayed a case of the jitters
By bulldozing through, in May, a Treason Act,
A classic case of how to overreact.
Then, in August, Lilburne published a broadside,
Giving Cromwell and Co. another rough ride:
An Impeachment of High Treason. You decide.
Was this folly (tantamount to suicide)
Or a blow for freedom? What can't be denied
Is that Lilburne displayed commendable pluck.
Nor was our fine firebrand down on his luck.

Rhyming History

His trial for treason caused a sensation,
Whipping the entire political nation
Up into a frenzy. The prisoner engaged
In shouting matches with the judges. Enraged,
They gave honest John as good as they got.
At one stage he called for a chamber pot,
And used it, in full view of his tormentors!
A motley lot, these unruly dissenters.

He could hardly have been prepared for what hit him.
When the jury declared (hurrah!) they'd acquit him,
Lilburne was hailed as a popular hero.
Was his legacy lasting? Well, sadly no.
He set up as a soap-boiler (this is true),
A spent political force. He couldn't do,
When it came to the crunch, what leaders have to:
Organise, stick to a plan, carry it through.
A visionary and an idealist,
He died disappointed and wasn't much missed.

Cromwell and the Commonwealth

Before we return to Ireland, kindly note:
Because of the kinds of pamphlets Lilburne wrote,
The Rump passed another Act, in late September,
Curbing the freedom of the press – this, remember,
From a government committed, allegedly,
To fundamental principles of liberty.
The poet John Milton, no less, was enlisted
As the leading censor. He should have resisted.

Just five years earlier he'd written an essay,
Areopagitica, which, I have to say,
Is perhaps the finest argument (to this day)
In defence of press freedom. "Give me the liberty,"
He wrote, "to know, to utter, and to argue freely,
"According to conscience." Well, I mean, really!
Hypocritical or what? See how rapidly,
How cynically, even great men come to grief.
That a poet should stoop so low. Beyond belief.

Cromwell's Irish campaign

Right, to Ireland at last. Am I resisting it?
Perhaps. If ever Cromwell stumbled, this was it.
When Fairfax declined the commission to command,
Oliver accepted it. Ever in demand,
A military hero, England's saviour,
Few were prepared for his ruthless behaviour.

Rhyming History

Ireland was in crisis. The emergency
Required drastic action. The insurgency,
The Irish rebellion, wanted quelling.
The words used by Cromwell are pretty telling.
He would pursue this "great work" (for such was his wish)
"Against the barbarous and bloodthirsty Irish".

Oliver was formally appointed, in June,
As Commander-in-Chief. An unexpected boon,
An unsought honour, was his nomination
As Ireland's Lord Lieutenant. "Abomination!"
Exclaimed the Catholics. Cromwell couldn't care less.
Though short of money and arms, he had to confess,
He was ready (nay, forced) to sail by July.

Catastrophe beckoned in Ireland. And why?
Dublin was almost entirely surrounded
By Ormonde's forces. This threat was compounded
By the parlous prospects of General Monck
In Ulster. The General, in a blue funk,
Capitulated, giving Cromwell cause to curse.
Affairs in Dublin were heading from bad to worse,
When gloriously the governor (Jones by name)
Won for himself no mean measure of fleeting fame
By breaking from the city and putting to rout
Ormonde and his cohorts. There's little room for doubt
That the tactics and courage of Colonel Jones
Eased Oliver's passage, of that I make no bones.

Drogheda

Cromwell landed near Dublin, now a 'free' city,
Then marched north to Drogheda where, more's the pity,
He laid most bloody siege. Further north lay Dundalk.
Ormonde, despite his reputation as a hawk,
Feared Cromwell penetrating too far up the coast.
What oily Ormonde, to be honest, dreaded most

Cromwell and the Commonwealth

Was a renewal of the lethal alliance –
Struck in a spirit of passion and defiance –
Between Ulster Catholics and the Commonwealth.
The Marquess (looking out, as ever, for himself)
Saw Drogheda therefore as a kind of buffer
Between Dublin and the north. That mad old duffer,
Sir Arthur Aston, with 2,000 men (at most),
Was deputed to hold the town. Soon he was toast,
Beaten to death with his own wooden leg, we're told.
Sir Arthur, poor fellow, was a sight to behold,
Torn limb from limb (though in his case with horrid ease).
The ghastly perpetrators believed, if you please,
That the false leg was stuffed with golden sovereigns.

"All's fair in love and war," they say. "Who dares, wins."
Wretched *clichés*, to excuse the worst of sins.

To Sir Arthur Aston's 2,000 men
Cromwell's numbered well in excess of ten –
Or twelve, by some accounts: 4,000 horse
And 8,000 foot. Oliver, of course,
Relied not just on numerical strength
But on the fact that he shared a wavelength
(Don't laugh) with God. No, it can't be denied.
Cromwell was sure the Lord was on his side.
The Almighty was as horrified as he
At the monstrous scale of the barbarity,
The wickedness and the profanity
Of the poor, benighted Irish. His mission
Or, as Cromwell perceived it, God's commission
Was to act as the honest instrument (no joke)
Of the Almighty's judgement on these needy folk.

Sir Arthur was similarly confident.
Drogheda's position was Heaven-sent:
Atop a high hill and strongly fortified
With a massive, thick wall. It were suicide,

Rhyming History

Folly at very best, to risk an attempt
To storm such a stronghold. Cromwell was exempt,
Of course, from folly – and not averse to risk.
His strategy was bold, its execution brisk.
His artillery was strong, his discipline tight,
Yet he did try at first (yes, I have got this right)
To take the town by peaceful means. Aston, he knew,
Had problems with loyalty, even (this is true)
With his own grandmother. She, one Lady Wilmot,
Sought to betray him. He gave as good as he got.
He drove her out of town, threatened to blow her up,
Family or not. A mere storm in a tea-cup?
Well perhaps, but such displays of disunity
Seldom pass, in time of war, with impunity.

Aston was stubborn (not unlike his gran),
A hot-headed, brash, impetuous man.
He refused Cromwell's summons to surrender.
There were known rules of warfare, remember,
Then as now. The so-called rule of 'no quarter',
Designed, some claimed, to prevent wholesale slaughter,
Sadly often had the opposite effect.

For no valid reason that I can detect,
If a besieged commander refused to yield,
But then failed to hold the fort, his fate was sealed.
Once the walls were breached and the position taken,
The victor won the right (if I'm not mistaken)
To put all combatants to death. It was too late
Then to run up the white flag and avert their fate.
A harsh rule, perhaps, but one meant to encourage
Sensible surrender, not misguided courage.
Whether it had this effect I've no idea,
And I've no intention of debating it here.
Suffice it to say though, Cromwell was furious
When Sir Arthur wouldn't give ground. What's curious
Is how the numskull could have failed to realise
Oliver's strength, there to witness with his own eyes.

Cromwell and the Commonwealth

Be that as it may, Cromwell's first assault
Failed to make an impact. Hardly his fault.
Drogheda's walls were strong, sturdy and thick
And Aston was prepared (this makes me sick)
To risk all, civilians included,
For his own glory. He was deluded
(Very) if he thought Cromwell would back off.
Sir Arthur, of course (I'm sorry to scoff),
Was wilfully blind, an arrogant toff,
Ready, he swore, to go to any lengths
Sooner than yield. One of Oliver's strengths,
On the field and off, was his persistence.
His next attack met with less resistance.

He led from the front, a bold thing to do.
Casualties numbered more than a few,
Not least, I'm afraid, on Oliver's side.
Now whether or not this dented his pride
I know not, but his fury turned the tide.

Rhyming History

Cromwell was angry. Many thousands died
In hot blood. Prepare to be horrified.
Women and children, offered no quarter,
Were hacked down at will: somebody's daughter,
Somebody's mother, wife, somebody's son –
Beloved of somebody, every one.

The priests of Drogheda fared worst of all,
With barely one left living by nightfall.
It was open season on Catholics
And, though we don't have detailed statistics,
Hundreds were put to the sword, have no doubt.
Most bloody deed. A massacre. A rout.

To the Lord Lieutenant (surprise, surprise)
This was the work of God. In Cromwell's eyes
Not only was Drogheda 'His' judgement
On the Irish, a fitting punishment –
So he wrote (in terms) to Parliament –
But the 'atrocity' (my word, please note)
Would "tend to prevent" (and now I do quote)
"The effusion of blood" in days ahead.
Cool words indeed after so many dead.

Dundalk and beyond

The awful irony, it has to be said,
Is that this aspiration proved largely true.
Dundalk to the north (the next in the queue)
Quickly succumbed without a fight; and Trim,
North-west of Dublin, likewise. Down to him,
Claimed Cromwell, and with reason. Folk were scared.
Towns fell like dominoes and thus were spared.

Good news from Belfast, and from Newry too –
Good news at least from Cromwell's point of view –
Meant Oliver could now move down from Louth
And focus his attention further south.

Cromwell and the Commonwealth

The port of Wexford, believe it or not,
Though small, was a possible trouble spot –
A harbour where they feared that the young King,
Charles the Second, might hazard a landing.
This was far from a probability,
But still a danger. Between you and me,
A matter of far greater urgency
Was the question of winter quarters.
Oliver would enter choppy waters
Were he stranded without a winter base.
Ireland can be a bleak and bitter place
In any weather. Autumn already,
Dry, warm quarters were a necessity.
Cromwell's men were hungry, weary and sick.
They needed shelter, they needed it quick.

Oliver expected, as well he might,
Wexford to yield to him without a fight.
Wrong! Its governor, one Sinnott by name,
Dug in his toes. Whether he was to blame,
Or Cromwell, for the subsequent bloodshed
Is a subject still hotly debated.
In Cromwell's favour, it has to be said,
Sinnott was constantly changing his mind.
To call him cunning is hardly unkind –
Devious, subtle, manipulative
And sly. The Lord Lieutenant, as I live,
Was a model of reason and fairness
Beside Sinnott, who showed no awareness,
Or so it appears, of the rules of war.
When Oliver speaks, don't show him the door!

Sinnott, the oaf, sought to negotiate,
Seeking "honest terms". He deserved his fate,
But his stubbornness sadly jeopardised
The good people of Wexford. I'm surprised,
Frankly, that Oliver was so patient.
Sinnott's duplicity was so blatant

Rhyming History

That he might have been given shorter shrift.
Cromwell showed great forbearance (it's a gift)
By agreeing generous terms, by which
The enemy could leave. Then came the hitch.

Before surrender terms had been agreed,
Events occurred to make poor Wexford bleed.
One Captain Stafford, a cowardly man,
Treacherous and shabby (I'm no great fan),
Betrayed the Castle, under his control,
To Cromwell. He sold Wexford (and his soul)
For his own safety, the wretch. The Castle
Adjoined the wall and was part and parcel
Of Wexford's stout and sturdy main defence.
Stafford's betrayal (a heinous offence)
Enabled Cromwell's frustrated forces,
Thousands of men, with weapons and horses,
To breach the great wall. They simply stormed through,
On the rampage. What could Oliver do?

As Commander-in-Chief, I'd say quite a lot!
These Irish, he reckoned, deserved all they got.
So Cromwell did nothing, this the foulest blot,
Worse even than Drogheda, on his career.
For there the town refused to yield. But here,
At Wexford, discussions were still under way
For an orderly exit. I'd have to say,
Were I asked, that Oliver blew it that day.
The killing was indiscriminate, wilful –
Civilians, combatants, clergy. Pitiful.

Oliver's negligent lack of interest
Was deadly and shameful. He never confessed.
He boasted, rather. The massacre was 'crowned'
(My word for it) when three hundred souls were drowned,
Trying to escape. Cromwell's sole professed regret
Was that Wexford (wait for it, you've heard nothing yet)

Had been rendered unfit by the wholesale plunder
For his little winter holiday. Small wonder
That after more than three centuries and a half
The Irish have still not forgiven this bloodbath.
Cromwell the great liberator? Don't make me laugh.

After Wexford he moved west to New Ross.
As if to show he wasn't really cross –
He was a family man, remember –
Cromwell accepted the town's surrender
Without gunfire or bloodshed. He agreed
Most reasonable terms. He guaranteed
Civilians freedom from injury,
A gesture of commendable mercy,
As well as letting all men under arms
March away scot free. One of Cromwell's charms
(You see, I'm a fair man) was honesty,
A sense of personal integrity.
If he promised people their liberty,

Rhyming History

He'd always honour his word. One request
However, he refused. Whether in jest
Or in earnest, the governor sought leave
For the folk of New Ross, can you believe,
To enjoy liberty of conscience.
Cromwell, God bless him, made little pretence
Of his contempt. The idea was crass.
He'd never allow the Catholic Mass.
Outlawed in England, so in Ireland too,
The Mass was ungodly, such was his view.
Freedom of thought, perhaps; but of practice, no.
Tolerance in religion? Some way to go!

The Commander-in-Chief fell ill at Ross.
Cromwell, of course, never ceased to be boss,
But he was plagued with fever (very weak)
And at times, we are told, could barely speak.
Fit enough again by late November
(Though still with no winter digs, remember),
He struck out for Waterford. However,
Discouraged by the ferocious weather,
He moved to Dungarvon, then on to Youghal,
Where he dug in for the winter, renewal,
And a well-earned bath. The season was cruel.

Just two months later he was back again.   **1650**
Kilkenny was a spectacular gain:
Ormonde country. Sir William Butler,
Governor, swore (he could have been subtler)
To hold Kilkenny whatever the price.
Not called on to suffer the sacrifice,
Butler was allowed to walk away free,
Despite his foolhardy obduracy.
A different story, don't you agree,
From Drogheda or Wexford? Cromwell, you see,
Was far more inclined, you can take it from me,
To justice and mercy than to cruelty.

His campaign nonetheless was far from complete.
Ormonde's force at Gowran went down to defeat.
This was in March. His officers were all shot.
Rules of war again: they deserved what they got.
His common soldiers, however, were spared.
They'd have been shot had they resisted. None dared.
Ollie was on a roll. Now he could afford
To indulge his foes. He couldn't at Wexford.

But he suffered a huge setback at Clonmel –
A rare, unsettling event for Cromwell.
His soldiers were lured into a cunning trap.
Oliver, waiting in vain at the gate, poor chap,
Was witness to the agonised screams of his men
As they were slaughtered. He prayed for their souls. Amen.

2,000 of his troops were massacred that day.
Yet he didn't wreak revenge. That wasn't his way.
Clonmel was unable to hold out for ever.
When it fell, Hugh O'Neill (slippery and clever),
Cromwell's adversary, had decamped. However,
Despite his fury at O'Neill's cowardly flight,
Cromwell showed mercy. To the citizens' delight
And, no doubt, to their considerable relief,
He imposed moderate terms. Now it's my belief –
The Irish among you will strongly disagree –
That Cromwell's name has been tarnished by history.
He could lose his cool. The instances are few.
One bad lapse can mark a man. That's nothing new.

Cromwell's return from Ireland

Oliver, not before time, was recalled
In May 1650. He was appalled.
He'd started the job, he was fighting fit,
He'd prefer to stay out to finish it.
But a conflict with the Scots was brewing,
A powder keg (this the young King's doing).

Rhyming History

Oliver was needed, his expertise,
His flair. Ireland, already on her knees,
Was all but conquered. Wasted overseas,
Cromwell returned, leaving his son-in-law,
Henry Ireton, to pursue the war.
The Irish campaign continued (it's true)
For three more years – till 1652.

England's hero was lauded like no other man
Since the story of our proud islands began.
That is something of an exaggeration
(You'll have spotted that), but the entire nation,
Rich and poor, high and lowly, young and old,
United in his praise. Heroic, bold,
Courageous... A day of thanksgiving
Was announced. The Irish, less forgiving,
Remained, as like as not, silent that day.

The poet Andrew Marvell had his say:

" 'Tis madness to resist or blame
" The force of angry heaven's flame. "

So Cromwell's campaign was immortalised
In his *Horatian Ode.* I'm surprised,
Indeed touched, by the poet's awareness
Of the late King's plight. His sense of fairness
Is compelling. Charles "bore his comely head"
(Vintage Marvell) "down as upon a bed".
Tender words for an arch-republican
And future MP for Hull. Quite a man.

Speaker Lenthall rose in Parliament
And spoke of Cromwell as "God's Instrument".
A telling phrase. We should respect Lenthall.
His words, dear reader... Well, they say it all.

Cromwell and the Commonwealth

The Scottish campaign

Young Charles, as we've noted, was proclaimed King
By the Scots. It was not to their liking
That his father had been prosecuted
By the English, and then executed –
Over their heads. Charles had been their King too.
Up north his murder caused quite a to-do.
The Scots took it badly. Well, wouldn't you?

Scottish Presbyterians, it would seem,
Despised the new republican *régime*
Established in England. They feared, not least,
Cromwell himself (as his power increased),
His radical beliefs and, one suspects,
His tolerance of religious sects.
They dreaded sectarian influence,
Did these Presbyterians. It made sense,
To the Scots, to woo their martyred King's son,
To restore him in Scotland and, that done,
To introduce throughout the entire realm
(England and Ireland too), with Charles at the helm,
Presbyterianism. Just like that!
Well, were Charles to oblige, I'd eat my hat.

I should have to! For that's what he agreed!
Hyde advised against it. Charles took no heed.
He lived for the moment, spurred on by greed.
If the Scots were ready to go it alone,
He was more than prepared to throw them a bone.
He'd embrace their religion. Once on the throne
He'd impose it on England, as one of their own.
Charles hadn't, of course, the slightest intention
Of keeping his word (I thought I should mention).

News of Charles' Scottish trip was the occasion
For Cromwell's prompt recall. The Rump feared invasion.

Rhyming History

Thomas Fairfax

Thomas, Lord Fairfax, who'd stayed as nominal chief
Of the New Model Army, resigned. My belief
Is that Fairfax was never fully reconciled
To the King's foul murder. A man who rarely smiled –
Take a look at his portrait, by William Fairthorne –
A more melancholy fellow had never been born.
Tall, swarthy (as a boy, 'Black Tom' was his nickname),
Sir Thomas (as he then was) won eternal fame,
At a critical juncture of the Civil Wars,
Battling for the Parliamentary cause.
Bravely he fought at Naseby in particular,
And later, courageously, at Colchester.

Fairfax was a moderate, though, in this regard:
Parliament served as the King's "greatest safeguard"
Against his enemies. He saw in monarchy
The best bulwark against chaos and anarchy.
When called to serve on the Bench at the King's trial,
He stayed away. Some thought he was in denial.
Not so. Fairfax was appalled at the whole process.
When his name was read out, Lady Fairfax, no less,
(In disguise, but it was she) exclaimed without fear,
Behind her mask: "He has too much wit to be here!"
No fool, Sir Tom! Yet he declined to intervene
In a plot to rescue the King. Nor was he keen,
To say the very least, on the sentence of death.
He appealed on Charles' behalf. He wasted his breath.
Don't infer from this that Fairfax was a weak man.
Hardly. But from the moment the trial began,
Events moved with inexorable energy.
All a man of honour could do, it seems to me,
Was sit out this sad, lamentable tragedy.

Fairfax was a true servant of the republic
For its first two years. The King's murder made him sick,
But Thomas was nothing if not realistic.

Cromwell and the Commonwealth

As we've seen, he avoided the Irish campaign.
His loss (if that's the right word) was Oliver's gain.
Now he retired altogether to Nunappleton,
In Wharfedale. I wouldn't exactly claim he had fun.
Consider that portrait! But he relished private life,
Looking after his horses, spending time with the wife –
Not, of course, in that order. Tutor to his daughter
Was Andrew Marvell, the poet. Just what he taught her,
I'm not exactly sure. But Fairfax could have done worse.

For Marvell composed some of his very finest verse
During his sojourn in Yorkshire (or so I'd suggest) –
The Garden, for example, surely one of his best:

"Society is all but rude
"To this delicious solitude."

This could only have been penned in a secluded place,
Where withdrawal from the wider world spelt no disgrace.

"Stumbling on melons, as I pass,
"Ensnared with flowers, I fall on grass."

Rhyming History

The swollen imagery! The voluptuousness!
The most noble of poets, I'm obliged to confess.
So be it. Let's leave him with Fairfax, his employer,
And rejoin Cromwell, warrior and destroyer.

Cromwell's arrival in Scotland

Our hero set sail from Youghal in late May.
His trip to Scotland was soon under way.
Charles had arrived there on the 10th of June,
With Oliver expected all too soon.
The English numbered 16,000 men,
A formidable force. The 'where' and 'when'
Of the engagement was the question.

Cromwell came armed with the suggestion
(Proposal, rather) that they avoid blood.
War, he averred, could be nipped in the bud
Were the Scots to lay down their arms (as if!)
And send 'King' Charles packing. A little tiff,
Nothing more. Cromwell was boxing clever.

He knew that religion, as ever,
Underpinned this dispute and he'd never
(I repeat, never) countenance the spread
Of Presbyterianism. That said,
He made some calculated overtures.
The Scottish Kirk, he conceded, had flaws,
Yet was highly esteemed and respected –
"Brethren", he called them. As expected,
The Scots were singularly unimpressed
By Cromwell's weasel words. He tried his best.
Was he in earnest? I've no idea.
But the Scots weren't having any! No fear!

Cromwell's plan was for a pre-emptive strike.
Haddington he reached (after quite a hike),

Cromwell and the Commonwealth

East of Edinburgh, by late July.
But it seemed too eerily easy. Why?
All became clear. However hard he'd try,
He couldn't tempt the Scottish army out.
Their David Leslie was, without a doubt,
A most skilled commander. Why pick a fight?
No point. Far better to keep out of sight,
Lie low, and let desertion, disease
And famine wreak all the havoc they please.

Dunbar

Not what the Lord General expected.
Once his pleas for peace had been rejected
He marshalled his troops and prepared for war.
Instead, he found himself waiting. What for?
Not much! The Scots under Leslie dug in,
While Oliver... Well, his patience wore thin,
As did his diminishing resources.
Men were falling sick; so were the horses;
Hunger, to say nothing of wet weather,
Drove Cromwell to the end of his tether.

He hazarded an ill-advised attack
On Edinburgh. This failed. He fell back,
In desperate need now of fresh supplies,
To Dunbar on the east coast. Hardly wise.
It surely should have come as no surprise
That he got caught. However the land lies,
To position yourself, effectively,
Between your sworn foe and the open sea,
Well... Call me simple, but it seems to me
That Cromwell, a fairly sensible chap,
Fell headlong into a terrible trap.

Where Oliver led, Leslie now pursued.
Cromwell was fraught and in a fretful mood.

Rhyming History

He'd fought himself out of many a spot,
But this was as perilous as it got.
The Scots boasted 22,000 men,
The weary English barely more than ten –
Heavily outnumbered by two to one.
There was no way on earth, under God's sun,
For Cromwell to dodge a crushing defeat.

The Scots were cocky though, far too upbeat.
Leslie's forces stood possessed of Doon Hill,
A prime location, and a bitter pill
For Oliver to swallow. However,
In a bold move (rash and far from clever),
Leslie (whose guns, it's true, were out of range
Of Cromwell's troops) ventured downhill. It's strange,
To say the least, that having made a start,
He then stopped! His men were in robust good heart,
Confident and strong. Victory was his
For the taking. Yet he blew it. Gee whizz!

The Scots, off-guard, settled down for the night.
The English go hang, tomorrow they'd fight.
Some officers even went off to sleep
In neighbouring hamlets. It makes you weep.
There they dreamt of their place in history,
And of driving Cromwell into the sea.

Oliver plucked triumph from adversity.
Leslie's lazy and lacklustre policy
Was bred of nothing but pride and vanity.
Even to think of his bed! Insanity.

As dawn broke on the 3rd of September –
A date I expect you, please, to remember –
Cromwell launched his astonishing attack
On the Scots' right flank. They couldn't hold him back.
Taken by surprise, their alarms (don't scoff)
Had been set for later, so hadn't gone off.

Cromwell and the Commonwealth

God, as usual, was on Cromwell's side.
"The Lord of Hosts!" the English soldiers cried
As they hacked through the enemy. A rout.
A massacre. Wholesale slaughter. Wipe-out.

3,000 poor Scots were slain by first light,
10,000 taken captive. Quite a night.
Twenty Englishmen were killed. That's twenty.
Not twenty thousand. Yes, you heard: twenty.
To their friends and families that's plenty;
Nonetheless, a negligible figure
Against the Scots, men of courage, vigour
And passion. Cromwell was ecstatic.
The Scots he claimed (a little dramatic)
Were made by God "as stubble to our swords".
Fine words are one of victory's rewards.

Dunbar was Cromwell's greatest achievement.
No Scot, of course, will be in agreement.
Yet to head off defeat, against all odds,
Was quite a feat (though the credit was God's).

Rhyming History

They say that Cromwell was so desperate to win
That he bit his lip till the blood ran down his chin.
It's more than an interesting conjecture –
Sorry, this isn't a history lecture –
What would have happened to the English nation
Had he lost. An earlier Restoration?
A third Civil War? In all probability
A decade of chaos, mayhem and anarchy.

Edinburgh and beyond

Dunbar left Cromwell broadly in control
Of most of southern Scotland. On a roll,
He took Leith and Edinburgh although,
For weeks, the Castle held out. No great blow.
He finally wore the governor down.
By Christmas Eve he was lord of both town
And Castle. Stirling, however, dug in.
Was this a war Cromwell just couldn't win?

He launched a spring campaign to conquer Fife,   **1651**
But failed, fell sick and nearly lost his life.
Doctors despaired, not for want of trying,
As it appeared their patient lay dying.
He'd reached a great age (he was fifty-two),
His strength was on the wane and this he knew.
Yet by June he'd revived, by God's good grace.
The fever had left him thin in the face,
And dysentery sore in another place,
But Cromwell bounced back. He couldn't care less
For earthly discomforts. God it was, yes,
Who'd summoned his spirit back from the dead:
"He hath plucked me out of the grave!" he said.

Cromwell's campaign in Scotland was put on hold
During his illness. Other factors, I'm told,
Played their part. His troops were left out in the cold –

Cromwell and the Commonwealth

I'm not just speaking metaphorically –
By Leslie's old 'come-and-get-us' policy.
These months were marked by lack of activity.
In July though, after Cromwell's recovery,
This all changed. John Lambert, a trusted deputy,
Won a crushing victory at Inverkeithing,
A small town in deepest Fife, due east of Stirling:
A much needed boost to morale, the perfect thing.
This opened the route to the north. For what it's worth,
Oliver advanced apace, not pausing till Perth.

The breakthrough was worth a great deal in fact.
Cromwell, with an instinct that Leslie lacked,
Developed a cunning new strategy
To flush out the King. Young Charlie, you see –
Who'd been crowned in January at Scone –
Was itching to invade England, and soon.
His nonsensical plan (call it a dream)
Was to gather support (a madcap scheme)
From disenchanted Royalists down south,
And this he trumpeted, the blabbermouth,
To all who would listen. Regrettably,
For him, one who did pay heed was Leslie.

Oliver now moved most of his army
North of Stirling. Some said he was barmy
To have left the lowlands undefended.
Well, exactly as Cromwell intended,
Leslie seized on this 'opportunity'
To march on England with impunity.
This wasn't simply an exit strategy –
A second winter up north, take it from me,
Would have proved a killer, quite literally –
But also a finely calculated trap.
Cromwell waited. Would it work? Charlie, poor chap,
Swallowed the bait. Cunning, Oliver's strongest suit,
Had served his purpose well. He set off in pursuit.

Rhyming History

Charles on the march

'Charles the Second' (self-styled) took the western route
Down through England. He needed now to recruit.
His ambition was to attract to his lists
Battalions of discontented Royalists.
Alas, it never happened. Charles got it all wrong.
Far from augmenting his force as he went along,
His progress was marked by a strange disinterest,
Inertia and cowardice. Put to the test,
The royalist party proved itself unready,
Uncommitted, unsupportive and unsteady.

Cromwell shadowed the King. Just enough rope
He gave him to hang himself. Charles, the dope,
His forces outnumbered by two to one,
Fetched up in Worcester. A man on the run,
He stood not a chance. His army was tired,
Demoralised, hungry and uninspired.
Cromwell took the decision to attack
Rather than lay siege. Though the King fought back,
With ferocity, the cause was soon lost.
He defended the city at huge cost:
Over 3,000 Royalists were slain.
To what purpose? I'm sure I can't explain.
Their bodies piled up in the alleyways,
Dead horses too, like one of those old plays,
Where corpses litter the stage in Act Five
And nobody seems to be left alive.

But this wasn't fiction, this was for real.
For me, such drama holds little appeal.
As for the lead actors, how did they feel?

Charles' flight

Charles fled the field. He was lucky, I'd say,
To escape with his life. As was his way,

He made light of the matter. Merry, yes.
How he survived… Well, that's anyone's guess.
He took to his heels. He was young and fit.
An oak tree, they say, played a part in it.
Inn signs to this day (this isn't a joke –
I dare say you've seen some, 'The Royal Oak')
Commemorate the occasion. Well said.
Less ominous than his dad's pub, 'The King's Head'.

A strange prediction

Worcester was fought on the 3rd of September,
Exactly a year to the day, remember,
Since Dunbar. They say that superstition
Dictated the date. Cromwell's position,
Outside Worcester, on the 2nd was strong.
He delayed for a day (I could be wrong)
To ensure that the battle fell on the date
Of his victory at Dunbar. Well, that's Fate –
Or is it, if the whole thing is pre-arranged?
There's an odd legend (was Oliver deranged?)

Rhyming History

That he led one of his captains, on the 3rd,
To a wood, where they met (I know it's absurd)
A strange old man who promised Cromwell, then and there,
That he'd "have his will" for seven years, then – despair!
Crazy, I know. Till I tell you (you have my word)
That Cromwell breathed his last on September the 3rd,
Just seven years later, in 1658.
It appears that the hermit told Oliver straight!

Be that as it may, Cromwell's great victory
Fully cemented his place in history.
He returned in triumph. "Our Chief of Men,"
John Milton hailed him. England cried, "Amen!"

New challenges

Cromwell never took to the field again
After Worcester. There was work to be done
In government, and it wasn't much fun.
Milton again, in the selfsame sonnet,
Recognised this and brooded upon it:
"Yet much remains," he wrote, "to conquer still."
The poet understood, for good or ill,
That "peace hath her victories" (all too true)
But that "new foes arise". This Cromwell knew.
The perils facing England were immense:
To take his place in government made sense.
London his base, he turned his attention
To affairs of state. Simmering tension
Subsisted, as ever, between the Rump
And the Army. Which way would Cromwell jump?

The very question oversimplifies.
To some this often comes as a surprise,
But Oliver was prone to compromise –
Within limits, of course. Pragmatic, wise
And far-sighted, he came to realise,

Rapidly, that an honest settlement,
Won with the minimum of discontent
From all parties – Army, Parliament,
Sectarians, old Royalists, the lot –
Was the one and only option, and not
(I repeat, not) further confrontation.
In short: not strife, but accommodation.

You can bet your life, Cromwell tried his best.
Never one to shirk the severest test,
He gave it his best shot. He failed, of course.
He had guts, the constitution of a horse,
Determination and that ruthlessness
Required of all heroes. Nevertheless,
After almost a decade of trying
The project collapsed, there's no denying.
Following his death it all fell apart.
How did this happen? Well, let's make a start.

The Rump's intransigence

The devil lay in the Rump's laziness.
There's a certain degree of haziness
Around this period. Records are slight
And most historians, try as they might,
Find themselves confounded by lack of facts.
I shall do my best. Hold on to your hats.

Cromwell desired the Rump to set a date
For its dissolution. Endless debate,
Cynicism and procrastination
Precipitated mounting frustration
Throughout the whole political nation.
The Rump's increasing prevarication
Angered the Army and, in Cromwell's eyes,
Was a threat to peace. He and his allies
Urged the Rump to prepare for elections.

What, though, if Oliver's expectations
Were not met – not only as to the date
Of the new poll, but its outcome? His fate,
He knew, could be adversely affected
Were the new House, as many expected,
To consist of members sympathetic,
Say, to the royalist cause. Pathetic!
Was he man or mouse? And that testy crew,
The Presbyterians, might prosper too,
A further danger. What could Cromwell do?

Risk it. Anything was better, he knew,
Than the corrosive continuation
Or, worse still, the self-perpetuation
Of this archetype of rank mismanagement,
This rotten, stale, remainder Parliament.

Two weeks after Worcester the first debate
Was held on dissolution. A firm date
Was set for elections – three years ahead!
Some progress! The Lord General saw red.
He himself had spoken persuasively
(Still a member of the Commons, you see)
Against the delay. A slap in the face.
A blow to his authority. A disgrace.

Cromwell favoured, up and down the nation,
A programme of reconciliation.
He supported a wide indemnity
For former Royalists, leniency
For those recreants who'd fought for the King.
The policy, though, had a hollow ring.
The Act of Oblivion excluded
A host of those it might have included.
Exceptions were made (for no sound reason)
For certain 'categories' of treason.

Cromwell and the Commonwealth

Well, most of those who'd fought against the state
Fell through the net. Their lands were confiscate,
Sold off to cover the Commonwealth's debts.

Since Royalists now posed very few threats,
This was short-sighted, as Oliver knew.
But the Commons had spoken. What could he do?

Oliver's discontent didn't end there.
Impatience gave way to gloom and despair.
In the summer of 1652   **1652**
He petitioned the House. Well, wouldn't you?
The vexed question of elections apart,
The list was lengthy. It came from the heart.
Ignorant ministers should be removed,
With only the godly being approved;
Soldiers' arrears should be promptly paid,
Provision for widows and orphans made;
Of equal urgency was law reform,
Cost (and lack of access) ever the norm;
Corruption and scandal; and much, much more,
Including (not least) relief of the poor.

Rhyming History

What (please take note) is often forgotten
Is that the Rump was not only rotten
But fundamentally conservative.
What Cromwell often found hard to forgive
(And could never forget) was that Pride's Purge
Didn't result in a radical surge.
Religious Independents, in force,
Made up large numbers and Cromwell, of course,
Approved this progressive and novel trend.
However, it didn't signal the end
Of the Presbyterian membership.
The latter, undoubtedly, lost some grip,
But were deeply entrenched, nevertheless.
The Independents, I have to confess,
Were a disappointment. Reforming zeal
They lacked, as well as popular appeal.

The Commons' innate conservatism
Held one virtue: stability. Schism,
Rife in the land at large, was kept at bay –
In the upper echelons, anyway.
Many in government were downright scared
Of the Army. They were therefore prepared,
At a price, to tolerate the delay
And muddle of the Rump, watch the decay
Of its revolutionary ardour
And protest from the touchline: "Try harder!"
Feeble. Inadequate. And regressive.

Religion

Here's an example (less than impressive)
Of the Commons' reactionary nerve.
Cromwell's religious, reforming verve
Had its limits, but his philosophy
Was based on tolerance, on liberty –
Freedom of conscience. Persecution,
By the state, was to him no solution.

Catholics, however, were excluded,
As were Anglicans. You'd be deluded
(As I was, before I read up on it)
If you thought anyone could benefit
From Cromwell's 'broad Church'. In a modern sense
It wasn't broad at all. This is quite dense,
A knotty area of history,
Even to specialists a mystery –
And certainly to me. I shall be brief.

As far as I can see, Cromwell's belief
Was in a loosely structured Church. No one
(No Protestant, at least) under the sun
Should be denied the right to seek God's will
In the scriptures. Perhaps you've had your fill
(I know I have) of this religious stuff.
It's all so convoluted. Fair enough.
Before we move on, I mentioned above
An 'example'. This I think you will love.
It illustrates, in one specific case,
How Cromwell could be miffed at losing face.

It was some years later, but still holds good.
If you're loth to read on, I think you should.

Naylor's case

James Naylor, a leading evangelist,
A Quaker and so-called revivalist,
Rode into Bristol sitting on an ass.
His conduct, inflammatory and crass,
Was accounted a horrid blasphemy
Re-enacting, as it did, Christ's entry
Into Jerusalem. In a fury –
With no hearing, neither judge nor jury –
The Commons sentenced Naylor (who'd a beard
And long hair so, by definition, weird)

Rhyming History

To be whipped, pilloried, branded with 'B'
(That's 'B' for Blasphemy: neat, you'll agree),
Bored through the tongue and imprisoned for life.

To Cromwell, this treatment cut like a knife.
He'd no great sympathy for Naylor's case
(Whose conduct he thought a proper disgrace),
But where, he asked, would such punishments lead?
What more indictments, perforce, might they breed?

"God deliver me from such liberty,"
He wrote (thus distancing himself, you see,
From J. Naylor), "if this be liberty."
For he feared that in sensible men's eyes
The Commons could well have been compromised.
He abhorred Quakers, and I'm not surprised –

Deeply subversive in those early days.
But what of other groups with gentler ways,
Baptists, for one, even Independents?
Cromwell questioned (he spoke very good sense)
Where this would end. "For might not Naylor's case,"
He put to some officers, face to face,
"Happen to be your case?" Where draw the line,
Was Oliver's point. An ominous sign.

Limited political progress

What of the Rump's achievements? There were few,
But nonetheless some. A brief overview
Must encompass, in 1652,
A declaration of war on the Dutch.
This didn't please Protestants overmuch,
Their fellow religionists. But still,
A jolly good trade war, for good or ill,
Was popular at home. Ever gung-ho,
The English loved a punch-up. Cromwell, though,
Saw the conflict as futile, expensive
And a folly, its damage extensive.

The vast sum of three hundred thousand pounds
Was laid out on the Navy, ample grounds,
I should hazard, for opposing the war.
For what in the end was the fighting for?
To revive English commerce, if you please,
By stopping Dutch vessels on the high seas
To monitor whether they broke new rules –
Imposed by the English themselves, the fools.
These outlawed goods from certain colonies
Being shipped from those same territories
Save in vessels flying the English flag.
Vain and idiotic (sorry to nag),
Though it should in fairness be pointed out
That trade did prosper, without any doubt.

The Rump were to be congratulated,
Their combative policy vindicated.

Other 'successes'? I'm scratching around:
To be perfectly frank, nothing profound.
After abolishing the monarchy –
A constitutional necessity –
And the House of Lords, what else did it do?
Tinkered with law reform. English, it's true,
Was the standard language now of the courts,
But justice, sadly, was still out of sorts.

Restoration of the monarchy?

Cromwell was obsessed with a 'settlement'.
In the eyes of some observers this meant
The reinstatement, in some shape or form,
Of a monarchy. He'd have caused a storm,
Particularly within the Army,
Had he floated anything so barmy
As a wholesale Stuart Restoration.
But the welfare of the English nation
Was the subject closest to Cromwell's heart.
Reform was urgent. So who'd make a start?
No one if not him, and Cromwell knew it.
How history may choose to construe it,
I care not, but he refused to rule out
A "mixed monarchical government". Doubt,
Distrust, denial… A dangerous age.

'King' Oliver?

Rumours abounded. Difficult to gauge,
But Oliver delivered quite a shock
To his friend and ally, Bulstrode Whitelocke,
Strolling one fine day in St. James's Park.
"What if a man," he asked (having a lark?

Hardly…) "should take upon him to be King?"
Scholars have argued till it's sickening
Around this chance remark. Had it the ring
Of a statesman of ruthless ambition?

For a man in Oliver's position
It was indeed a daring thing to say.
Historians debate it to this day.
We shall never know. Bulstrode, anyway,
Was sole witness to the conversation
And only dropped his bombshell on the nation
In his *Memorials*, thirty years later.
Now don't ask me (I'm just the narrator),
But I should be quite surprised (nay, amazed)
Had Cromwell eyed the crown. He'd have been crazed
Even to think he'd get away with it.
He was able, intelligent and fit,
But frankly I think he'd have run a mile
Rather than be King. It wasn't his style.

A few years later they offered Cromwell the crown.
King Oliver. Just think of it. He turned them down.
Doesn't sound much like vaunting ambition to me –
Rather a man of substance and humility.

More trouble from the Rump

Reserves of patience were running low.
Parliament, the Rump, would have to go.
To expel it unilaterally
Were a massive risk politically.
As late as March (it's 1653),   **1653**
Cromwell contrived to persuade the Army
To back off this misguided policy –
Holding the balance as before, you see.
Notwithstanding, matters came to a head
The following month. It has to be said

Rhyming History

That history is hazy (yet again)
On the 'whys' and 'wherefores' (I've searched in vain)
Of Oliver's actions. Nobody knows
His exact motivation. Still, here goes.

For months the Rump had prevaricated
Over the vexed issue (which they hated)
Of elections. It comes as no surprise
That one key sticking point was the franchise.
In Cromwell's view, were elections too 'free'
(Hardly what we'd call a democracy),
The country might return 'neuters' (his phrase)
Or Presbyterians. England's malaise
Was bred of those who'd forgotten the wars,
Were blind to truth and hostile to the cause.
To return power to such renegades
Were to inflame matters further, in spades.

Talks... and more talks...

Perhaps impossible of solution,
The problem focused on dissolution.
The Rump was reluctant. Cede its powers?
Not likely. Discussions lasted hours –
Days, weeks, months... Now, when talks go on for years,
Something has to give or it ends in tears.

Cromwell (and the Army) favoured a lull –
This is important, sorry if it's dull –
Between the dissolution of the Rump
And a new Parliament. Quite a jump!
The proposal was relatively new,
But Oliver and others (quite a few)
Believed that regular Parliaments
Posed a threat to England's liberty. Nonsense,
Of course, to twenty-first century ears,
But the rotten Rump had fuelled such fears

Cromwell and the Commonwealth

Of inertia, abuse and reaction
As to stir, in the 'progressive' faction,
The demand for a strong executive
To promote godly reform. As I live,
This was a most uneasy compromise,
A distinctly dangerous enterprise:
'Executive' meaning who? No surprise
If Cromwell and his cohorts spring to mind –
Though selfless to the last, I think you'll find!

On the 13th of April, at long last,
A Bill was introduced. The die was cast,
It seemed, for elections. Events moved fast –
Faster, indeed, than Cromwell bargained for.
Key questions were still unresolved. Therefore,
Over the next few weeks, meetings were held
Of importance perhaps unparalleled
In our constitutional history.
Precise details remain a mystery,
But Cromwell, Army and Rumpers discussed
Endless provisions (all dry as dust),
Including the vexed franchise question
And, vitally, the new suggestion
Of some kind of temporary council
To take over from the Rump, to fulfil
All the functions of government until
(Whenever that might be) new elections
Gave rise to men's better expectations.

The talks were inconclusive. They adjourned
For further discussions. Then Cromwell learned,
To his amazement, the following day,
That the Rump had reconvened. I must say,
For sheer gall their conduct takes the biscuit.
I'm staggered they were ready to risk it,
Given Cromwell's fiery reputation.
A shiver of dread passed through the nation.

Rhyming History

No one crossed Oliver. Something was wrong
And Cromwell knew it. He'd been strung along.
The Rump were demonstrating their contempt
For the agreement they'd struck. Their attempt –
Arrogant, hasty, ham-fisted, futile –
To second guess Cromwell missed by a mile.

Oliver's fury

As soon as he heard of their treachery
(There's no fitter word), with celerity
He strode down to the House. Ready to burst,
He took his seat. He was quiet at first,
Attentive as the Rumpers spoke their worst.
When he rose to speak, it was hard to tell
If his strategy was planned. Silence fell.
His tone was measured. Ominously calm,
His demeanour gave no case for alarm.
Dressed quite simply (he'd had no time to change),
He commended the Rump (now this was strange)
For their good offices. He did his best
(Or did he?) to be cool. But in his breast
The fury was mounting, simmering rage.
The squeamish among you should turn the page.

Cromwell lost it. Remember Drogheda,
Its citizens so much cannon fodder?
This was a Drogheda moment. He spat,
He ranted, he raged, he roared. After that,
He bellowed and cursed. He snarled and he swore
(Though he didn't blaspheme). He kicked the floor.
Drunkards, he called them, and whoremasters. Then,
To widespread dismay, he called in his men.
Forty armed musketeers, marshalled outside,
Stormed the Chamber. I'll leave you to decide:
Was this not political suicide?
What might John Pym have made of it? The King
(Remember poor Charles the First?) did nothing

Cromwell and the Commonwealth

(I repeat, nothing) as reckless as this.
But Oliver was deranged. Hit or miss,
Cromwell made his mark. William Lenthall,
The Speaker, was hardly happy at all
To be dragged from his chair and ejected.
I don't suppose he ever expected,
As the Commons' Speaker in '42,
To star in another such scene. Would you?

Certain plucky members remonstrated,
To no effect. Others hesitated.
Cromwell's honesty was called into question,
His morality even. The suggestion
Merely stoked Oliver's anger. The mace
He ordered to be removed. A disgrace.
This represented (as it still does today)
The Speaker's authority. Take it away

And the Commons is defunct, extinguished.
The Rumpers – the lowly, the distinguished –
Were homeless. Cromwell was nonetheless told
By John Bradshaw (this was frightfully bold)
That Parliament could only be dissolved
By itself, so the issue stood unresolved.

After the Rump

What next, then? Where did the power now lie?
With Cromwell, of course. He sought to deny
That this was ever his aim, fighting shy
Of absolute authority. The fact,
However, remained: with the Rump now sacked,
Oliver was boss. He behaved with tact.
He acknowledged, freely and openly,
That, as Lord General of the Army,
Ultimate power resided in him.
This he didn't claim lightly, on a whim,
But as simple truth. He expressed unease,
Deep discomfort at this and, by degrees,
Sought to devolve his power to others.

A group of like-minded men, his 'brothers' –
Fellow officers, if the truth be told –
Forgathered in haste. Their quest was twofold:
For an active, interim government,
And for some kind of long-term settlement.

A new Council, established by Cromwell,
Addressed the former and addressed it well.
The business of government, day to day,
Continued quite smoothly, I have to say –
To Oliver's credit. More urgent, though,
Was the settlement. More elections? No.
The only acceptable solution,
To safeguard the fruits of revolution,

Was a body made up of nominees
"Called by God to rule with him", if you please
(Cromwell's own words), a chosen Assembly
Invested with supreme authority,
Comprising those of godly quality.
A Council of Officers chose the men,
All one hundred and forty of them, then,
Once 'selected', Cromwell left them to it –
A hopeless task, and most members knew it.

The 'Barebones' Parliament

Yet Oliver's hopes were high. His address
To the new Assembly was, I confess,
Well over the top. An embarrassment.
His plea for liberty was eloquent:
Freedom of conscience. It was well meant
But, as politics go, highly naïve.
"Love all the sheep," he urged (can you believe?),
"Love the lambs, tender all and cherish all."
He spurred them on (as far as I recall)
To allow "the poorest Christian soul…
"The most mistaken…" (he was on a roll)
To live "peaceably" and "quietly"
A life "in godliness and honesty".
All very well, but less a policy
Than a sermon. Leaders should never
Preach morality. Never. Ever.

The Assembly proved itself quite unfit
For the challenge. 'Barebones' some christened it,
The 'Barebones Parliament'. One member –
One of the few we ever remember –
Was a Baptist preacher, 'Praise-God' Barebones.
His name, with its ironic overtones,
Was adopted by Cromwell's enemies
To cast scorn on his folly. By degrees

Rhyming History

The weakness of the Barebones Parliament
Became sadly apparent. To some extent
(Limited, true) there were certain successes.
It curbed a range of unpleasant excesses
In the care of 'idiots' and lunatics;
And though, of course, there's a dearth of statistics,
Civil marriages were legalised,
Resulting in large numbers solemnised.

Other more modest reforms in the law
Were also accomplished. So why, therefore,
Did the Barebones Parliament collapse?
A lack of reforming zeal? Well, perhaps…

Tithes

No. Tithes. These were how the clergy were paid,
Some of them, anyway. Protests were made –
And had been, indeed, for centuries past –
At this 'one-tenth tax'. Aspersions were cast
By the taxpayers, charged at ten *per cent,*
As to where the levy finally went.
For many lay rectors, so it appears,
Staked a claim to these tithes, over the years,
For their own private use, stoking grave fears
Of civil unrest. It could end in tears,
With some clergy even out on their ears.
Not only did this cause widespread dismay,
Your average peasant just couldn't pay.

Be that as it may, tithes were associated
With landowners' rights and were hotly debated.
The sad, short-lived Barebones Parliament comprised
A number of radical sects, well organised,
Albeit a minority. Few realised
Their strength until they scared the moderates to death
By voting against tithes. They should have saved their breath.

Cromwell and the Commonwealth

Rather than risk defeat at the radicals' hands –
Such as Fifth Monarchists and other 'rebel' bands –
The moderates (led by John Lambert) engineered
The Assembly's dissolution. As Cromwell feared,
The Barebones Parliament fell short of the task.

On tithes, where did Oliver stand? Since you ask,
He was a life-long traditionalist,
A conservative to the core. Get the gist?
As a landowner he too was terrified
Lest land law in England should become 'de-tithed'.

The maximum life of the Assembly
Had been set at eighteen months. By then, you see,
Social ills were to have been corrected,
Law and morality fully respected,
And godly reform (so Cromwell expected)
Complete. New candidates could then be selected
And a truly moral Assembly elected.
All this to happen within a year and a half –
A revolution in manners. Don't make me laugh!

But the Barebones Parliament, as we have seen,
Collapsed within five months. How was Cromwell so green?
He put his faith in the Lord, as simple as that.
If God takes sides in politics, I'll eat my hat.
Cromwell himself confessed that the doomed Assembly
Was the product of his own "weakness and folly".
It posed a threat to "liberty and property",
With never a hope of governing properly.

So, on December the 12th, 1653,
Members of the Barebones (well, the majority)
Voted themselves dissolved (quite voluntarily)
And relinquished to Cromwell their authority.
They delivered the mace, as was appropriate,
Into Oliver's hands. But the radical set

Had been bounced and bamboozled. They weren't finished yet.
They were frantic and furious, deeply upset,
Suspecting a set-up, a political fudge.
They were right. So they sat there. They stayed. Wouldn't budge
(Some of them, anyway). What did Oliver do?
He summoned the muskets. Again. Well, he had to –
Though this time their numbers were mercifully few.

The Lord Protector

From December the 16th (quick, you see)
Cromwell would sign himself 'Oliver P.' –

Oliver Protector. Events had moved
With lightning speed. Cromwell was approved
(By whom? That's a well-directed question)
As Lord Protector. There's no suggestion
That he sought the crown. King Oliver? No.
Cromwell was sensible enough to know

That the Army would never have worn it.
Nor would Royalists at large have borne it.
And Cromwell's objective, as we shall see,
Was to foster peace and stability,
Reconciliation and harmony.

His inauguration ceremony,
Having said that, reeked of regality.
Oliver was soberly dressed, in black,
But the pageant around him took folk back
To the coronations of yesteryear,
Where splendour and pomp raised many a cheer.
His only concession to frippery
Was a deep-gold hat band! His modesty
Was palpable. His air of gravity,
His sense of purpose and solemnity,
Were manifest and plain for all to see.
The ancient emblems of monarchy
Set off his natural simplicity.

The *Instrument of Government*

The new Lord Protector's authority
Derived (speaking constitutionally)
From the *Instrument of Government,*
Drawn up by John Lambert, whose intent
Was to draft a single document
Containing one clear, honest statement
Of the Head of State's governing powers.
The document must have taken hours,
But when it appeared in its proper form
The *Instrument* took the country by storm.

Where was power vested under the *Instrument*?
Provision was made for a new Parliament
To exercise legislative authority
Jointly with the Lord Protector whose wings, you see,

Rhyming History

Were thus clipped from the start – at least in theory.
One unexpected, shared responsibility
Was the so-called 'disposition' of the Army.
At first blush, Cromwell's authority would appear
To have been strictly curbed. He had no cause to fear.
The *Instrument* was biased in Cromwell's favour.
Just a few examples should give you a flavour.

Parliament (according to the *Instrument*)
Could be dissolved after a mere five months. This meant
That the body in whom this power was vested
Wielded huge influence. Now, no one suggested
(God forbid!) that Cromwell wrote in this provision,
But the fact remains that it was his decision,
As Lord Protector, and his decision alone
To dissolve Parliament, and this was well known.
All he had to do was simply pick up the 'phone
(Anachronism, sorry) and dismiss the lot
If they snubbed him. And he gave as good as he got,
Demonstrating again to a wary nation
His deep sense of outrage, despair and frustration.

This time, though, no need for muskets! This was the law.
What else, he would argue, was the *Instrument* for?

In addition, not only could Cromwell dismiss
His Parliament at will, but (listen to this)
He only need summon one every three years.
Do the maths for yourselves. There were very real fears
That in the thirty-one months (did you work it out? –
The maximum) of parliamentary drought,
The Protector could turn into a dictator:
Sole executive head and sole legislator.

The *Instrument*, luckily, did its level best
To qualify these doubts and set men's minds at rest.

Cromwell and the Commonwealth

A Council of State was duly constituted
To exercise (this is rather convoluted)
Executive powers in conjunction, again,
With the Protector. This might have occasioned strain
Had not the Council consisted (surprise, surprise)
Of Oliver's supporters. What few realise,
However, is that a modest minority
Of Cromwell's first Council (out of fifteen, just three)
Were of the Army. He was sensitive, you see,
To the charge of 'government by military'.

Be that as it may, the truth of the matter
Was Cromwell's vast authority. I flatter,
I dare say, but his sheer dynamism,
His massive personal magnetism
And his towering character, all these –
Sometimes cited as vices, if you please –
Eclipsed all vain constitutions. Taken together,
They sustained the Protectorate, whatever the weather.

Forget not, the Army stood four-square behind him.
The odds on outwitting the Protector were slim.

Cromwell's character

Moreover, he was appointed for life.
'His Highness', Cromwell became; his good wife,
Elizabeth, the 'Lady Protectress'.
They moved to a wildly fancy address,
Whitehall Palace. Cromwell couldn't care less
For pomp and show, though I have to confess
He did look forward to his weekend haunt,
Hampton Court, whence he would savour a jaunt
To Bushy Park for his recreation –
Hunting and hawking. His reputation
As a spoilsport was quite unjustified.

Rhyming History

For Noll had a warm, convivial side.
He loved music. This must be qualified.

Music in a religious context:
Definitely 'out'. But any pretext
To enjoy it as a secular art –
Proof, if need be, that he did have a heart –
Singing, for instance, was most surely 'in',
As was chamber music. It was no sin
To relish melody. The violin
(I've read this) grew in popularity
During the Protectorate. So you see,
He was no Philistine. A committee
Was even constituted (since you ask)
For the advancement of music. The masque –

Cromwell and the Commonwealth

The rage, you'll recall, in the old King's day –
Crept back into fashion, though the stage play
Was outlawed during this period. Dance,
Tending to vice and popular in France,
Was tolerated up to a degree
Within the bounds of strict morality.

The Protectorate Parliament

I'm straying away from my central text.
Under the *Instrument*, what happened next?

It wasn't till September '54,   **1654**
Over eight months later (this I deplore),
That the first Protectorate Parliament
Met with the Protector's blessing. This meant,
Of course, an interval of government
By Oliver (as *per* the *Instrument*)
And his buddies, *viz.* the Council of State.
They settled some business, at any rate,
Much of which, I'm afraid, was pretty dull.

The Council took advantage of the 'lull'
To make some marked progress on law reform –
Wills and probate, for example. The norm,
Sadly, in the justice process (as now)
Was delay and obfuscation, and how!

The Council made inroads (modest, it's true)
Into some of these problems. Of the few,
One was a new table for charging fees
By lawyers who were trying, if you please,
To benefit from stretching out their case
With jargon and gibberish. A disgrace.
No lawyer would hazard this trick today –
Good Heavens, no! It's simply not their way!

More importantly, and with good reason,
Only cases of murder and treason
Were now to attract the death penalty.
Hitherto, to a revolting degree,
Any adult or child (terrible times)
Could be put to death for trivial crimes.
A lesser reform, I should have you know,
Was a strict ban on growing tobacco –
This to protect the new economies
Of the country's emerging colonies.

The Dutch

But Oliver's policy overseas
Was, of all the Protector's legacies,
The most impressive. Cromwell's energies,
Twinned with his diplomatic expertise,
Brought to an end the first of the Dutch wars.

A popular (and patriotic) cause,
Oliver frankly had never been keen.
What was the point, he asked? Well, as we've seen,
To protect trade (so the argument went)
And to break the Dutch. Fine, to some extent,
But these were faithful Protestants, our 'kind'.
It offended Cromwell, I think you'll find,
To wage war against his fellows. So he,
With resolution and integrity,
Negotiated peace terms with the Dutch.

Both warring nations had rather lost touch
With their old objectives, if truth be told.
'King' Charles, moreover, had gained a toe-hold
In the United Provinces. The Dutch,
Under the peace, had to rid him of such
By agreeing to exclude his in-laws,
The House of Orange, from office. Few wars,

Of course, are anything but expensive,
Wasteful and cruel. Something has to give.

The Treaty of Westminster, at a stroke,
Deprived the King-in-exile (and his folk)
Of Dutch support. The Navigation Act –
The cause of the conflict (and that's a fact),
A tedious, tiresome, tortuous war –
Was endorsed at last by the Dutch. They saw,
As well as anyone else, that free trade
Was how the fortunes of nations were made.
Moreover the course of the war, sadly
(From their perspective), was going badly.
They were forced, then, to treat. Compensation
Was paid too. Oliver's reputation
Grew accordingly. There's no ignoring,
Cromwell's stock throughout Europe was soaring.
He signed commercial treaties by the score.
Freundschaft and *amité*: better than war!

Religious toleration

One policy greatly to Cromwell's credit
(Often ignored, so I'm glad to have said it)
Was that of religious toleration.
His interest in a unified nation
Was best served by keeping to a minimum
State interference. Only the troublesome
(Such as the Quakers) or the more quarrelsome
(Such as the Ranters) or the more meddlesome
(Such as the Fifth Monarchists) were kept at bay.
Their anti-social views, I have to say,
Rendered this disruptive fringe beyond the pale.

The Protector fought these zealots tooth and nail,
Though even Oliver (bless his cotton socks)
Would engage the Quaker leader, one George Fox,

63

Rhyming History

In private debate. Cromwell was a sinner,
Declared George over an intimate dinner!

He even struck up (though this sounds fantastic)
An earnest friendship with a great Catholic,
Sir Kenelm Digby. This was rated a sin
By that irate Puritan, William Prynne.
But Cromwell relished Sir Kenelm's company
And inclined to an engaging clemency
Towards Catholics. Freedom of conscience
Was Oliver's ideal. It simply made sense.

It should still not be forgotten, however,
That under the law Catholics would never
(I repeat, never) enjoy the liberty
To express their faith freely and fearlessly.
In practice, though, little was done to enforce
The anti-Catholic laws unless, of course,
There was evidence, or even suspicion,
Of mischief, rebellion, plots or sedition.

Cromwell and the Commonwealth

In addition, Cromwell re-admitted the Jews
To England. His Council held different views,
But he simply overruled them. Good for him!
This sound policy wasn't made on a whim.
The Jews had been driven out as long ago
As 1290, a most bloody blot, I know,
On England's historical record. Cromwell,
Never loth to deliver the odd bombshell,
Recognised their value and, down to this day,
The race has proved him right, I'm happy to say.

Cromwell's liberalism, as we shall see,
Was to cause not a little difficulty
When his first Protectorate Parliament met.

But I'm not quite ready to move on to that yet.
In the meantime a modicum of state control
Was imposed over religion. Cromwell's goal,
And that of his Council of State, was to ensure
High standards among the clergy. Above the law?
No longer! A commission was established,
With standards as rigorous as one could have wished,
To test and scrutinise the suitability
Of every candidate for the ministry
And all incumbents to boot. Schoolmasters, no less,
Were subjected to the same gruelling process.
Some were appalling; others no worse than expected.
Those deemed unworthy of their calling were ejected.

As for state interference, that was the lot
When it came to Church affairs. Oh, I forgot,
Sorry… To end on a far more positive note,
There was one further reform that would win my vote.
The income of the poorest clergy (very low)
Was increased, though there was still a long way to go.
Funds were there, of course, but I still say, fair enough.
The government showed some willpower. All good stuff.

Rhyming History

The Sealed Knot

What could Royalists do to stop the rot?
Sadly (from their perspective) not a lot.
One secret society, the Sealed Knot –
A rag-bag of dissident Royalists,
Catholics, disaffected loyalists
And mad mavericks – was in existence
By 1654: a 'Resistance'.

John Thurloe

To restore the monarchy, by armed force,
Was its dreadful mission. It failed, of course,
Not least owing to the good offices
Of John Thurloe. They were all novices,
These Sealed Knot fellows (at this stage at least),
But Thurloe was not. The son of a priest,
And trained in the law, he served for eight years
Loyally, calmly (no sweat and no tears),
With a diligence that was consummate,
As Cromwell's sole Secretary of State.

All the business of the Commonwealth
(Or most of it) he knew. Thurloe himself
Exerted no influence, however,
On policy as such. Thorough, clever,
And fiercely committed to the cause,
What earned for John his enduring applause
Was the tight-knit, well-run network of spies
That he recruited. Thurloe's ears and eyes
Were everywhere. And it's no surprise,
With royalist rumblings on the rise,
That such a system of intelligence
Was a necessity. It made sound sense.

Home and abroad, from Dublin to the Hague,
His spies would sniff out trouble. Never vague,

Cromwell and the Commonwealth

He was ever focused and alert. No,
Nothing suspicious got past Thurloe.

The part of his policy that helped most
Was his crafty censorship of the post.
Civil libertarians will cry foul
But Thurloe, in truth, was a wise young owl.
Imagine the chaos generated
Had Oliver been assassinated.
The end in this case amply justified
The means. Had Lord Protector Cromwell died,
What then? In February the Sealed Knot
Aborted at an early stage a plot
Against the state. Then John Gerard, in May –
Not a Sealed Knot member, I'm bound to say –
Conspired to ambush Cromwell on his way
From Whitehall to Hampton. Thurloe took note
And Oliver wisely travelled by boat.
Gerard was duly arrested and tried.
The verdict was guilty. The traitor died.

Rhyming History

More trouble with Parliament

Time at last. On the 3rd of September,
The third anniversary, remember,
Of Cromwell's famous Worcester victory
And (his favourite date in history)
The fourth of his great triumph at Dunbar –
This, surely, a coincidence too far –
The Protectorate Parliament met,
The first of two. The stage was surely set
For a most glorious future and yet,
Inside five months, the Parliament failed.

All Cromwell's best hopes were sadly derailed
As the new Commons proved themselves surly,
Obstructive and stubborn. All too early,
Within days of their convening in fact,
The anti-Cromwell contingent attacked.
In advance, a handful of Royalists
Had been weeded out of the Commons lists
(Effectively debarred) by the Council
As men lacking integrity, sound will
And (a bit odd this) "good conversation".

These exclusions caused no consternation,
Within the Council's powers (as they were)
Under the *Instrument.* Quick to occur,
However, were moans concerning the range
Of the Commons' own authority. Strange,
Given that it had been well understood
That the *Instrument of Government* should
(Nay, must) be a 'given', above debate.
All of a sudden to negotiate
Its terms… Well, way beyond the pale. Cromwell,
Whose high hopes knew no limits, truth to tell,
Was appalled. In his opening address
He'd called for "healing", and laid extra stress

Cromwell and the Commonwealth

Upon the need for "honest settlement".
He boasted of the solid achievement
Accomplished to date by the government.
They were met together, Oliver swore –
His eyes were moist, his emotions were raw –
On the greatest day that England had seen,
Ever! How could Cromwell have been so green?

The twin pillars of his goodly intent
Were acquiescence in the *Instrument*
And a fair measure of toleration
In religion: a strong foundation
For a settlement for all the nation.

He was fast disappointed on both heads.
A number of 'new' members were 're-treads' –
A quarter from the Long Parliament,
Including one most irksome opponent
In the shape of Sir Arthur Haselrig.
A troublesome Puritan, who talked big,
He was one of the famous Five Members
'Named' by Charles the First. No one remembers
(Few anyway) what became of him then.
He proved an adequate leader of men
In the great Civil War, but got the hump
When Oliver Cromwell dismissed the Rump.

Arthur harboured a healthy suspicion
Of despotic power. His position,
In the best 1640s tradition,
Was that Parliament should enjoy control
Over the Army. Given, on the whole,
The Army's contempt for Parliament,
This was a non-starter. To some extent
We should sympathise. For there's little point
In a joint power that's only half joint!
Under the *Instrument* the power lay
With Commons and Cromwell. But come the day

Rhyming History

(And the day came) when Oliver dismissed
Parliament and… well, you get the gist.

Adding further insult to injury,
The Commons upset the military
By planning to downsize it, severely,
For reasons (of course) of economy.

A mere nine days after its first meeting
The Commons saw Cromwell back, his greeting,
On this occasion, rather more frosty.
Their opposition was to prove costly.
The fundamentals of the *Instrument* –
The blocks, as it were, of a settlement –
Were non-negotiable. Four key points
Were sacrosanct. Frankly, what disappoints
Was the Commons' utter intransigence.
For Oliver's policy made good sense:
One, the definition of government
As one person and a Parliament;
Two, the clear principle of liberty
Of conscience in religion; three,
A shared control over the armed forces;
And four, Cromwell's right (horses for courses)
To dissolve Parliament, this latter
To prevent the Commons growing fatter
By a kind of self-perpetuation,
A risk to the political nation
Perceived in the dying days of the Rump.

Roughly eighty members opted to jump
Rather than sign a forced 'Recognition'
Endorsing Cromwell's entrenched position.

But those who stayed proved ever obdurate.
Recognition of the Protectorate
Was to prove illusory. Yet again
The Commons attacked, with all might and main,

Cromwell and the Commonwealth

Cromwell's hold over the Army. Old hat,
I know, but my word how they balked at that.
On moral issues such as blasphemy,
Licentiousness and profanity,
They prepared to remove Cromwell's veto
Over Commons' bills. Acceptable? No.

John Biddle

John Biddle's case brought matters to a head.
A Unitarian, it must be said
That Oliver had precious little time
For Biddle and his ilk. His dreadful crime,
To the mind of the Commons committee
That examined his case, was heresy.
His denial of Christ's divinity
Elicited minimal sympathy,
Not least from Cromwell. The verdict (guilty)
Was no surprise. But what price liberty?
Wherein lay the Commons' authority,
Moreover, to try a heretic's case?

The entire process, a perfect disgrace,
Alarmed and offended the Protector –
Both, I should hazard, in equal measure.
Though Naylor's case (which came later) was worse,
John Biddle's, no less, was 'freedom averse'.
Biddle's books were burnt and his punishment
(Kinder than Naylor's) was imprisonment.
Oliver arranged, the least he could do,
To pay him an income (yes, this is true)
Of twenty-six pounds a year (his money,
His very own), ample testimony
To his charity, his humanity,
And his honest good sense. Heresy? Pooh!
Live and let live. The Commons, in his view,
Were showing their true colours: obstructive,
Wayward, perverse and counterproductive.

Cromwell's fury

Cromwell concluded he'd been sold a pup.
Once the statutory five months were up **1655**
He dismissed the Commons. He'd had enough.
Some members jibbed at this and cut up rough,
For Cromwell, in truth, had cheated a bit.
The dissidents claimed they'd a right to sit
For five calendar months. Cromwell said no:
Five lunar months. The crafty so-and-so!
Evidence again (should you need to know)
That Oliver, with the 'force' behind him,
Called the shots. Cock of the walk, sink or swim.

Cromwell was livid. For only recently
Had these same men contested their liberty
With the bishops. Horrible hypocrisy
It was, wilfully, selfishly, now to be
The oppressors. Settlement and harmony
Were a sham. Division and discontent
Thrived by this miserable Parliament.

Penruddock's uprising

Twenty hectic months were to run their course
Before Cromwell was moved again, perforce,
To summon a second Parliament –
And hectic they were. One early event
Of note was a royalist uprising
Led by John Penruddock. What's surprising
Is that this was the only major plot
That got off the ground, believe it or not,
In all these precarious years. Cromwell
Had been highly successful, truth to tell,
In 'softening up' the opposition
In ways that bolstered his own position.

He scrapped the hated Oath of Engagement,
Thus putting an end to the 'estrangement'
Of those men who refused to recognise
The death of monarchy and the demise
Of the House of Lords. In this he was wise.
He sought to stop old wounds "fresh a-bleeding"
By setting out (and largely succeeding)
To mitigate the divisive impact
Of seizures of royalist lands. In fact,
He perceived himself as a champion
Of the old social order – "noblemen,
"Gentlemen" (Oliver's words) "and yeomen".
Zealots who strove to abolish such ranks
(Like the Levellers) he labelled as cranks.
Equality of wealth for all? No thanks!

Small wonder, then, that support was lukewarm
For royalist rebellion. The storm,
Such as it was, did no damage at all:
Hardly a hurricane, more of a squall.
John Desborough, at Oliver's behest,
So-called Major-General of the west,
Was despatched to deal with Colonel John.

Deal with him he did. The rebellion
Started when Penruddock took Salisbury –
Though please don't take 'took' too literally.
He began by setting the convicts free
From the city's gaols. Between you and me,
Ex-cons don't make perfect soldiery.
Be that as it may, having decided
Not to hang two judges (and derided,
Roundly, for his pitiful cowardice),
Penruddock took hostage (listen to this)
The sheriff, still in his nightshirt and cap.
He suffered, I'm told, no further mishap.

Rhyming History

Now at the head of some four hundred men,
Penruddock marched west. Seven out of ten
(My estimate) were drunk, the other three
(Of this I've been assured, reliably)
Past military age or half-asleep.
The Marquess of Hertford, the little creep,
Promised support, a pledge he didn't keep.
Others (enough to make you want to weep)
Likewise 'forgot' to materialise,
As poor Penruddock came to realise
(Shock and awe) that he was doomed. Then came word
That Desborough was on his way. Absurd,
I know, but Colonel John still ploughed on
Towards that royalist stronghold, Taunton.

Stronghold, alas, no more. Help was long gone.
The gates were shut against him. Tiverton,
His next port of call (a picturesque spot),
Where honest John gave as good as he got,

Cromwell and the Commonwealth

Was also, most sadly, his Waterloo.
I'm always glad (I don't know about you)
To witness a man, no ifs and no buts,
Fighting for a cause. Penruddock had guts,
Though the war he fought was utterly nuts.

Cromwell, sensibly, tempered his fury.
His wisdom prevailed. A local jury
Accorded Penruddock a fair trial –
Something of a risk, there's no denial,
With a local panel's reputation
For undue leniency. The nation
Held its breath. Justice was done, however,
As John was convicted. What was clever
(Politic too) was his head was chopped off.
This was more than merciful (no, don't scoff),
Given the usual alternative –
A ghastly fate I can never forgive,
Altogether far too eye-watering –
That of hanging, drawing and quartering.

The Major-Generals

Penruddock's revolt, though, had raised the stakes
And led to one of Cromwell's rare mistakes.
The Major-General 'experiment',
So-called, precipitated discontent
Not only with Royalists countrywide,
But with Englishmen at large. You decide:
Was this military innovation
A success, or simply a negation
Of all that Cromwell was seeking to do
By way of settlement? I'm asking you
Because, for once, I'm sitting on the fence.

To tighten up security made sense,
You bet it did. Penruddock's uprising
Was snuffed out, but it's hardly surprising,

Rhyming History

With rebels out to overthrow the state,
That Oliver sought to consolidate
His defence force, locally at any rate.
Eleven Major-Generals-designate
Were commissioned. Desborough was one
(The first in office), his place in the sun
Already guaranteed; another one
Was John Lambert; Cromwell's own son-in-law,
Charles Fleetwood, another. What were they for,
These Major-Generals? To keep the peace,
Of course – a sort of military police.
Local militias, under their sway,
Were to hold the royalist threat at bay.
So far, so successful. The endeavour
Was far more complex than this, however.

Firstly, the economy was ailing.
One of the reasons why it was failing
Was the heavy and ill-conceived expense
Of England's standing Army. It made sense
To cut it down to size, reduce the cost,
And to compensate for the numbers lost
With new militias, locally run,
And a darned sight cheaper, every one.
Some thought that the Army would throw a fit,
But they seemed quite relaxed and swallowed it,
Though don't ask me why. The new arrangement
Was financed, to general amazement,
By a 'decimation' tax. Royalists,
Those folk identified as loyalists,
Were assessed on their lands at ten *per cent*:
Divisive and unjust. Some settlement!

The Major-Generals, wherever they went,
Met with rancour, ill will and discontent –
Not just from Royalists. Part of their brief
Was suppression of vice (beyond belief)

And encouragement of virtue. Cock fights,
Race meetings, bear baitings, stage plays, late nights
(I'm joking), taking the Lord's name in vain,
Ale houses (you think I'm kidding again –
I'm not), brothels, gambling dens: all these,
Along with using swear words, if you please,
Fell within the comprehensive remit
Of the Major-Generals. This was it,
In Cromwell's eyes: the opportunity,
Finally, to supplant profanity,
Drunkenness, blasphemy and vanity,
With virtue, piety and godliness.

It ended in the most ungodly mess.
Don't tell me you're surprised. The one good thing
To come from this flop was a deep loathing,
Entrenched in our country to this very day,
Of rule by militia. Hurrah, I say!

In a word, the Major-Generals failed.
Royalist plots might well have been derailed,
But elections to the next Parliament
Only served to illustrate the true extent
Of opposition to the experiment.
The ten *per cent* tax was roundly rejected
And the Major-Generals, as expected,
Fell by the wayside. In words that still amaze,
Lord Protector Cromwell spoke up in their praise.
They were persons of "known integrity"
(Hard to argue with that) and "fidelity".
Men had enjoyed a year of "tranquillity"
Under their governance. Be that as it may,
The whole hopeless system was soon swept away.

Trouble with Spain

Was Cromwell losing his touch? I confess
That a quarrel he picked with Spain, no less,

Rhyming History

Met with conspicuous lack of success.
In the old tradition of good Queen Bess,
He singled out Spain as the enemy –
Keeping the French on side quite cleverly –
By seeking a fanciful guarantee
Of the right to trade freely, if you please,
In Spanish territories overseas,
Particularly in the West Indies.
English citizens in such colonies
Should be granted the liberty (mark this)
Of Protestant religious practice.

These demands were as red rags to a bull
To the Spanish King: dishonourable,
Disrespectful and intolerable.

The 'Western Design'

Nevertheless, Oliver sought, by force,
To implement his will. His terms, of course,
Were mad and this he knew. Hostility
(No word more apt) was his foreign policy,
Justified (as so often in history)
By national pride, self-interest
And vain hopes. Cromwell did his level best
To argue his case before the Council.
Many opposed him, but his iron will,
As ever, prevailed. The 'Western Design',
So-called, marked a significant decline
In his confidence. Yet he was gung-ho:
Set sail for the Indies and fight the foe!

The plan was to transform, effectively,
Each and every Spanish colony
Into a new English dependency,
Protestant to a man. The Catholics
Would get a bloody nose. That's politics.

Cromwell and the Commonwealth

The expedition was doomed from the start.
All began in apparently good heart.
Cromwell had been advised that the Spanish
Were weak. One surprise assault, they'd vanish!
Hispaniola (the modern Haiti)
Was said to be ripe for attack, you see –
Easily taken. Cuba would be next,
Another soft target. Any pretext,
It seems, for arrogant optimism
Was seized upon. The accepted wisdom
Was this: within the space of two short years
(In time of war, it's often what one hears)
All of Spanish Central America
Would be ours. A spectacular error!

The expedition had two joint leaders.
I hardly need point out to my readers
That this was a recipe for chaos.
Fighting a campaign? You should know who's boss.
Robert Venables was the General;
William Penn was named as Admiral.
Neither man was markedly decisive –
Penn was weak and Venables divisive.
The fleet was ill equipped. The crew, I've read,
Were little more than a rabble: ill bred,
Ill disciplined, ill nourished, underfed,
Woefully ill prepared and, as I've said,
Destined, like headless chickens, for chaos.

First port of call: the Isle of Barbados.
This, as luck would have it, happened to be
A rare West Indian dependency
Of the English. The master plan, you see,
Was that Barbadians should seize, gleefully,
This glorious, golden opportunity
Of risking their lives for Admiral Penn,
General Venables, their whey-faced men…

…Sorry, didn't I say? Eight out of ten
Suffered most terribly in the tropics.
The 'runs' aren't one of the common topics
Expected in an epic *History*.
The cause, however, was no mystery:
They gorged on soft fruit, bananas and such,
Melons and oranges – far, far too much.

Their tummies rebelled. They hadn't a chance.
Their farts could be heard as far off as France.

Back to the plot. Most Barbadians refused
To play ball. In the main they felt ill used,
Bounced, bullied and patronised – nay, abused.
A few hundred mavericks volunteered
To join the rabble. But the King of Spain's beard,
For the record, wasn't even lightly singed!
Venables, from what I've read, was unhinged
And Penn little better. They could agree
On nothing. They'd no sense of strategy.

Their lack of competence was frightening,
Bedevilled, as they were, by infighting.
Hispaniola was the goal. At least
They'd fixed on something. The tensions increased,
As it now became progressively clear
That Penn had not the slightest idea
Where to disembark. He landed his men
In the most unpromising of spots, then
Was put out when Venables blamed him (Penn)
For the subsequent *débâcle*: a rout,
For which the two 'big chiefs', without a doubt,
Shoulder the prime responsibility.
Hundreds died, quite unnecessarily –
Over a thousand, according to some.

When the news reached him, Cromwell was struck dumb.
This was the first defeat that he'd suffered.
God was angry. In time he recovered,
More certain then ever that the liberty
Of the Protectorate, its prosperity,
England's very survival as a nation,
Depended upon moral reformation.
Was Hispaniola God's punishment?
"We have provoked the Lord!" Some statement!

The terrible twins, I have to confess,
Lived to enjoy one surprising success.
They took Jamaica. This was no hard task,
Being poorly defended (since you ask).
Within a week of their landing, in May –
It's still 1655, by the way –
The Spanish had surrendered, easy prey.

Jamaica remained (almost to this day)
A British colony. I'd have to say,
Were I a fan of rapacious conquests,
That Jamaica was a plum. It suggests

Rhyming History

That Venables might have been forgiven,
Along with Penn. Not so. Both had striven,
According to their own lights, for glory –
And achieved it. A different story
When Cromwell read it. Thousands had perished.
Although Jamaica came to be cherished
In years hence, Oliver cared not a jot
For this alleged triumph. Like it or not,
Lives had been lost through gross incompetence
And dire leadership. He made no pretence
Of his blind anger. The blame rested squarely
With Venables and Penn. Somewhat unfairly
(In my humble view) both were sent to prison,
The objects of scorn, contempt and derision.
This, of course, was the Protector's decision.

So was the Western Design in the first place.
To pass the buck thus was a perfect disgrace.
That's what leaders tend to do, isn't it?
I'm beginning to learn this, bit by bit.

Tax

There's further evidence, around this time,
That Oliver was sadly past his prime.
He overreached himself in *Cony's case*,
His strategy shameful, shabby and base.
George Cony, a merchant trading in silk,
Objected (as did others of his ilk)
To the charging of an import levy
On his goods. The penalty was heavy.
He declined, politely, to pay his fine
Before ejecting (I'd say well in line)
The officers who had stormed in to seize
His property. For his pains, if you please,
He was clapped in prison. Cony argued,
Most courteously (he was seldom rude),

Cromwell and the Commonwealth

That since Parliament wasn't sitting
It was oppressive and hardly fitting
(Nay, illegal) for Cromwell's government
To impose taxes. A sound argument.

Oliver made clear he thought otherwise.
But what caught the people most by surprise
Was the extreme force of his reaction
When Cony appealed his case. This action
Unsettled the Council, and Cromwell too –
So much so that Cony's counsel (this is true)
Was ordered, upon pain of imprisonment,
To drop the case! Is this what justice meant,
Protectorate-style? Conduct, I should say,
Worthy of Charles the First. It was his way
To impose taxation willy-nilly.
For Cromwell to do so? Just plain silly.

Or was it? As Oliver himself said
In a different context (this I read):
"If nothing should ever be done but what
"Is according to law" (this says a lot)
"Then the throat of the nation may be cut
"While we send for some to make a law." But,
I hear you object, but... er... what about
Parliament... the Rule of Law... ? Scream, shout,
Register all the discontent you will,
The stuff of government's a bitter pill,
With brute force ever in the repertoire.
It was maybe going a tad too far
To harass the lawyers. One who saw this
Was honest Rolle, the Lord Chief Justice,
Who refused to concede, so left office.

To return to the substantive issue,
Taxation, what else could Oliver do?
Let Cony get away scot free? Would you?

Rhyming History

Of course not. Funds had to be raised somehow.
Taxes were unpopular, then as now.
The Commons were idle through their own fault –
Remember their crude, full-frontal assault
On poor Cromwell. Taxes on silk, on salt,
On soap were essential, on hops, on malt –
The economy else would grind to a halt.

Spain

The Spanish King was cross (surprise, surprise).
Jamaica's loss, in his unbiased eyes,
Was a plain case of naked aggression.
A highly prized and precious possession,
The island's seizure could only mean war.
Cromwell edged closer to the French, therefore,
By means of a crafty trade alliance
Which drove an effective wedge between France
And Spain. One significant side effect –
And one which Cromwell could only expect –
Was that this in turn drove the exiled King
Into Spain's embrace. Cromwell was laughing.
The Spanish, he knew, were perfidious,
Artful, double-dealing, insidious
And corrupt. Any treaty that Charles made
Would be wholly worthless. He'd be betrayed.

So it transpired. Spain, apparently, pledged
To back Charles' restoration. It's alleged
(Who are we to doubt it?) that in return
He'd cede Jamaica. People never learn.
Greed, deception – it was all too absurd,
And it seemed that no one believed one word.

Admiral Robert Blake

Spain. The ancient enemy. Cromwell
Had no problem, as far as I can tell,

Cromwell and the Commonwealth

Gathering support. Nothing like a scrap
To bring a nation to heel. "Sterling chap,
"Old Noll. Always thought so. As for that Blake,
"Fantastic fellow, the finest since Drake!"

Robert Blake was a towering figure
Who ran the Navy with vim and vigour.
At the most unlikely age of fifty
He'd been appointed 'General-at-Sea' –
In sole charge of the Commonwealth Navy.
Blake's experience hitherto, mainly,
Had been the Army, in the Civil Wars,
Fighting for the parliamentary cause.
Born in the very same year as Cromwell,
The two had much in common, truth to tell.
Both returned early from university
Following their fathers' deaths. For Blake, you see,
Like Oliver, was a family man.
He was also a fervent Puritan
And an ardent, lifelong Republican.

His army record was second to none.
Many a battle in the west was won
By his courage and fortitude. Taunton,
Bristol, Lyme: the odds against were immense,
Yet all succeeded in their stout defence
Against the Royalists. Blake made his name
In these rigorous campaigns. But his fame,
His lasting glory, he achieved at sea.

He'd never been a sailor – honestly!
He may have ventured abroad once or twice
On business (I can't be that precise)
But he'd not held any naval command:
Never been asked, I suppose – no demand.
Be that as it may, Blake single-handed,
As if a new Sir Francis had landed,

Rhyming History

Revolutionised the Navy. Blake
Suffered no fools, allowed no give and take.
Effort was the watchword: blood, sweat and tears.
Over the course of the next seven years
New Articles of War were introduced
And a strict code of discipline produced.

In the early years of the Commonwealth
Blake lost no time in excelling himself
In battles at sea against Royalists.
This most canny of naval strategists
Routed young Prince Rupert, ever fighting
For his uncle's lost cause. Most exciting!
The late King's Navy, as a fighting force,
Was as good as destroyed. Rupert, of course,
Being Rupert, battled on for a while,
But in vain. He was beaten by a mile.

Then came the first Dutch War in '51,
With a host of victories. That war won,
Blake saw off pirates round the English coast
And further afield. Foreigners were toast!
He'd never take sides politically,
For his blunt, no-nonsense philosophy
Was this: it was, he declared, "not for us
"To mind state affairs" (he hated the fuss)
"But to keep foreigners from fooling us".
He'd no agenda save a battle plan
And a strategy. A fine, fighting man.

The Lord Protector backed him to the hilt.
A record number of warships were built
And English influence as far away
As southern Europe began to hold sway –
Its impact felt still to this very day.
The Rock of Gibraltar, for goodness sake,
Is British (you know this). That's down to Blake.

Cromwell and the Commonwealth

So, when Oliver's war with Spain began,
The Navy was strong and Blake was the man.
The Spaniards were up to their old tricks,
Plundering gold. In 1656   **1656**
(In September) the Spanish treasure fleet
Was intercepted and destroyed. Some feat!
Their entire force was wiped out, at great cost,
As galleons, gold and cargo were lost.
Blake thanked God for this famous victory –
Another trait, co-incidentally,
That he shared with Cromwell. It wasn't Blake
In command that day. He had a headache.
Captain Richard Stayner took the credit.

Still, it was Blake's campaign and he led it.
Through the winter he kept up a blockade
Of the Spanish coast. Huge fortunes were made
The following April, at Tenerife,
When the venerable Blake, like a thief,
Launched a daring assault on Santa Cruz,
Sinking sixteen Spanish galleons. Strewth!
Blake lost no ships. A little miracle.
He did lose fifty gallant sailors; still,
Set against all the Spaniards who died,
Who cared a fig? I'll leave you to decide.

Rhyming History

Such was the daring for which Blake's renowned.
Yet, as his flagship entered Plymouth Sound,
He died of the fever. Mortality
Misses no man, however great he be.
Blake was buried in Westminster Abbey,
A giant of his age, a true hero.

His journey, though, still had some way to go.
This may be something you won't want to know,
But come the Restoration his remains
Were dug up again and flushed down the drains.

Another Parliament

Spanish hostilities required hard cash.
Oliver solved this problem with *panache*.
One remedy that he strongly opposed,
Which the Council of State, I'm told, proposed,
Was 'extra-parliamentary' –
A poor solution, I think you'll agree –
Namely that well-worn chestnut, taxation
Without recourse to representation.
Cony's case was one thing, but Cromwell saw
No great virtue in financing a war
By indirect means or dubious law.
The decimation tax had failed to raise
Its expected revenue. Beyond praise
As the Major-Generals were, they'd failed.
Local taxes, the grief that they entailed,
And the new militia… well, let's say
That men were relieved when they fell away.

In a nutshell, the Protector required
Another Parliament. He aspired,
Still, to religious toleration
And widespread moral regeneration –
Neither, by any means, inconsistent
With a call to arms. Few were resistant.

Cromwell and the Commonwealth

Cromwell was pushing at an open door:
Folk loathed the Spanish and loved a good war.
Elections offered legitimacy
To Cromwell's campaign although, as we'll see,
The outcome was unsatisfactory.

But that's for later. All went well at first.
The Major-Generals were fit to burst,
Keen and confident. They quite failed to see
The depths of their unpopularity.
All except one were duly elected
To the new assembly, as expected.
They enjoyed, after all, a high profile.

But other new members, the rank and file,
Represented, to a deadly degree,
A threat to Oliver's authority:
Presbyterians, crypto-monarchists,
Independents, assorted Royalists –
A dreadful trend! Under the *Instrument*
(Remember that?) this new Parliament
Was purged. Just like that! The Council of State,
Aware, perhaps, it might soon be too late,
Barred over one hundred members – again
As not "God-fearing" (it's like a refrain)
Or "of good conversation". Fifty more
Declined to sit. Sorry to be a bore,
But out of some four hundred elected,
That's well over one third 'de-selected'.
Cromwell still argued the process was free.
It's hardly what I call democracy.

This 'pruned' Parliament quickly approved
Funding for the war. Cromwell was unmoved,
However, by the Commons' rejection
Of the Militia Bill, a confection
Of clauses drafted to perpetuate –
Or renew for a while, at any rate –

Rhyming History

The much derided decimation tax
And the Major-Generals. The attacks,
On all fronts, were lethal and Oliver
Kept his counsel. Who was he to demur?
He praised the Majors, but without a doubt
They caused a storm he could well do without.

New members took their seats in September.
Peace reigned at first. Then, late in December,
The bubble burst. Someone you'll remember,
James Naylor, caused a right royal rumpus
By entering Bristol (a rare old fuss)
Astride an ass. I told you this before –
I know, I know, I'm a terrible bore –
But this deed, a hideous blasphemy,
Whipped up the Commons to a fierce frenzy.
Righteous to a man, they judged him guilty
And poor James Naylor was branded with 'B'
(For Blasphemy, keep up), bored through the tongue,
Thrashed and pilloried (he wasn't that young)
And imprisoned for life. A foul disgrace!
Cromwell protested. "Might not Naylor's case,"
He opined, "happen to be your case?" But,
Sadly, he spoke up in vain. A hard nut,
This Parliament. What authority
Had the Commons to try poor James? Beats me.
They had none at all. What price, liberty?

A fellow of rare compassion, Cromwell
Arranged for a nurse to visit Bridewell
(Naylor's gaol) with physic and medicine –
A Quaker woman, no less. Naylor's sin
Was weighty and grave in Oliver's eyes,
But this gracious gesture was no surprise.

The Naylor case sharpened the Protector's mind.
Events were moving on. He was far from blind

To one imperfection in the *Instrument,*
Namely a single-chamber Parliament.
A proposed new Constitution was in draft
That commanded his support. He wasn't daft.
A restored second chamber (nominated –
By whom, I wonder?) was quickly debated
And approved. A new House of Lords. No protest
Was entered by Cromwell. His best interest
Was served by this 'check', this 'balance'. No contest.

The Humble Petition and Advice   1657

What he found harder to stomach was the rest.
'The Humble Petition and Advice', so-called,
Offered Oliver the Crown. He was appalled.

Or was he? King Oliver the First! The Crown!
Most tempting of temptations. He turned it down.

Rhyming History

Scholars have argued until blue in the face
As to Oliver's motives. In the first place,
Some reckon, he dreaded the reaction
Of the energetic Army faction.
John Desborough (one of Cromwell's in-laws)
And Charles Fleetwood (another) led the cause –
Against. Heroes, both, of the Civil Wars,
And two of Oliver's staunchest allies,
They viewed the monarchy with jaundiced eyes.

Yet Cromwell still came close to acceptance.
The Army had led him a merry dance,
Often, but never did Oliver blink.
Less in hock to officers than you'd think,
Cromwell was his own man. He sacked Lambert,
For example, and though this must have hurt
(Lambert, I mean) he was far from afraid
Of the consequences. Leaders are made,
Not born. They have to know when not to flinch,
To hold their nerve, when not to give an inch.

Cromwell was such a man. We have to look
Deeper for his motives. Many a book
I've read and I'm none the wiser. The Crown,
If accepted, might have caused a showdown
With the Army. There's no way of knowing.
As it was, there was to-ing and fro-ing
For months. The case was remarkably strong
For a King. Not my view (don't get me wrong),
But that of some. The whole system of law
Was based upon it. History, therefore,
Habit and tradition, were better served
By kingship. It's what the people deserved,
It's what they expected, it's what they knew.
Cromwell acknowledged this. What should he do?
Recent attempts at assassination,
Moreover, had unsettled the nation.

Cromwell and the Commonwealth

Were the next effort to be successful,
Who would inherit? Worrying. Stressful.

The very notion of a 'Protectorate',
Some claimed, was transitory and weak. And yet,
As Cromwell argued, the country was strong,
And respected abroad. Why right a wrong
That didn't exist? A sound argument.
His hobbyhorse – "healing and settlement" –
Might well be put at risk (far from clever)
Under a King. His life-long endeavour,
The honest pursuit of reformation –
In morals, religion, education –
Could be frustrated and overshadowed
By a return to the old forms. He owed
(Cromwell knew this) his place in history
To godly reform. It's no mystery,
Therefore, that his refusal (when it came)
Was a resolution made in God's name.

Oliver never sought personal fame.
The Crown was a mere "feather in a hat",
A toy, a trifle. We must believe that.
Yet had acceptance reflected God's will,
He'd have gladly succumbed. A bitter pill?
No. He was reported to be merry
On the day that he resolved it, very!

The issue had not been hard to decide.
He'd merely to ponder the regicide,
Charles the First, his decline, his bloody fall.
The Lord, of course, had been behind it all.
God had declared against the monarchy –
Not the late, beheaded King personally,
Nor even the Stuart royal family,
But the title itself: King. He "blasted" that –
Cromwell's own choice of word. I shall eat my hat

Rhyming History

If Oliver had any other reason.
Kings, crowns, orbs and sceptres. All out of season.

However, though still plain Lord Protector,
He won the right to name his successor,
This in the interests, I imagine,
Of stability. Not a sovereign
But, in the eyes of many, as good as!
He was invested with great razzmatazz –
Purple robe lined with ermine (all that jazz),
A sceptre of pure gold (I kid you not),
A sword of state, and other regal rot,
Even a 'coronation chair', so-called,
A throne in all but name. Aren't you appalled?
The whole thing reeked of rank hypocrisy,
Though all quite harmless, surely you'd agree.

Little new here, constitutionally.
A period of drift, quite frustratingly,
Set in. Oliver was in wretched health.
He scarcely acknowledged this to himself,
Yet for years he had been far from robust
And, as a man approaching sixty must,
He was forced, with reluctance, to slow down.

A new 'Upper House'

But not before yet another showdown
With his Parliament. The new session
Was to teach Cromwell a nasty lesson,
Bitter and awkward. When the Commons met,
In early '58, the stage was set   **1658**
For a battle royal. Cromwell had lost
The right to vet membership, at great cost.
Those members most opposed to the *régime*,
Excluded before, held in low esteem
Not only the man, but also his dream

Of an Upper House. These men, crucially,
Viewed a second chamber with hostility –
A real threat to Commons' independence,
And in Oliver's pocket. All this made sense.
The House of Lords, the 'Upper House' (what you will),
Consisted (imagine a more bitter pill)
Of sixty-three of Cromwell's nominees.
These embraced his son-in-law (what a wheeze),
His brother-in-law (today it's called sleaze),
His chum Bulstrode Whitelock, his own two sons,
General Monck (one of the heavy guns)
And even (great heavens) his ex-landlord!

The Commons dismissed

This was a folly he could ill afford.
Not surprisingly they turned against him –
The Commons, I mean. As if on a whim,
He stormed to the House in a terrible rage –
Just how much was planned isn't easy to gauge –
And dismissed the lot. He'd done it before,
He could do it again. His son-in-law,
Charles Fleetwood, meeting him, urged him to stop,
Pause for a mo before blowing his top,
Only to be brushed aside, a "milksop" –
Insulting indeed. So then, as needs must,
Another Parliament hit the dust.

Age, ill health and sorrow plagued Cromwell now.
Within a year he'd take his final bow.
His beloved daughter, Elizabeth,
Suffered from cancer and drew her last breath
But a month before her father, his death,
Some fancied, hastened by this tragedy.
The dismissal, though, in February
Of the Commons was evidence (you'll see)
Of one final outburst of energy.

Rhyming History

Rumblings in the Army against his rule
He swiftly addressed. Cromwell was no fool.
He assessed the risk and moved fast. Fleetwood,
No less, mustered all the support he could,
As officers whose loyalty was in doubt
Were disciplined, or simply thrown out.

'Our Chief of Men' ruled, most folk agree,
By naked force of personality.
In a word, there was no alternative –
Until his death, when something had to give.

Victory over Spain

The Protector's reputation was buoyed
By triumphs overseas. Cromwell enjoyed,
Late in life, considerable success –
In league with the French, though, I must confess –
Against their common adversary, Spain.

At great expense (more money down the drain)
Not only was Jamaica defended
(As God, I take it, always intended),
But Spain's dominance was all but ended,
To her King's great rage, in the Netherlands.
Dunkirk, we're told, fell into English hands,
The very first foothold the country had
In mainland Europe for years. Can't be bad.
All this did wonders for Cromwell abroad –
Despite the cost, which he could ill afford.

One eye-catching fact that can't be ignored:
James, Duke of York, fought on the side of Spain
In this awkward nightmare of a campaign.
A most almighty publicity *coup*
For old Noll Cromwell. What a thing to do!
What folly! What lunacy! Breathtaking!
Imagine, for the brother of the 'King'

Cromwell and the Commonwealth

To wage war against the very country
He was born to rule. The words 'gum-tree'
And 'up' spring to mind. Do forgive me –
I'm touched with a fit of levity.
Mad or what? But that's the Stuarts for you.
When Royals go crazy, that's what they do.

Sickness and death

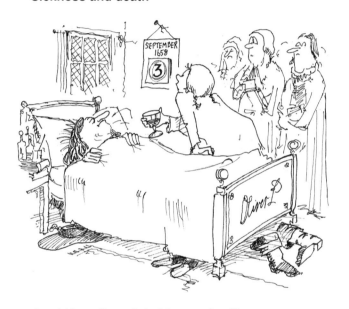

An old hermit predicted (remember?)
Long before, on the 3rd of September
(1651), that on the same day,
Seven years on, Oliver would die. Hey,
It's a good story. Superstitious rot,
Cry the historians. Like it or not,
On the anniversary of Dunbar,
And Worcester too, Noll Cromwell, superstar,
Was called to Heaven to meet the good Lord.
Some coincidence! You can ill afford

Rhyming History

To be completely cynical, you know.
Cromwell enjoyed no choice. He had to go
When Fate decreed. Not so very absurd
To take the aged hermit at his word.

What was the cause of death? Malaria,
Picked up in the general area
Of Ireland, scene of his famous campaigns?
The illness (one of its more gentle strains)
Was not uncommon in those far-off days,
Plaguing its victims in various ways –
Sweating and fever, distemper and fits,
Enough to drive a man out of his wits.
To kill him, though? Yes, perhaps. But Cromwell
Had recovered before, so I've heard tell,
So why not again on his deathbed? Well,
As I've hinted, his resistance was low,
He was old… In short, we shall never know.

Ollie suffered too from the dreaded 'stone',
Which was hugely painful, that much is known.
They discovered his spleen livid with pus
When they opened him up. He made no fuss,
Brave to the last. He placed his total trust
In the Lord his God, as he knew he must.

He named his successor, but only just!
His Secretary of State, John Thurloe,
Was one of many who needed to know.
He feared deep divisions, and that's a fact,
Were Cromwell to die without an heir. Tact,
However, and more than a little fear
Prevented him bending the old man's ear.
His boss was in a state of denial,
I'd hazard. It wasn't Oliver's style
To raise the mirror to mortality.
He was forced to confront death, finally,

Cromwell and the Commonwealth

By his Council, of which a select few
Forgathered at his bedside (they all knew)
And mooted the name of his eldest son,
Richard. This didn't please everyone,
But Cromwell assented. So it was done.

"Heaven's Favourite!" Who could disagree?
Andrew Marvell: spot on. His poetry
Was in a state of sad decline, frankly,
But his lines on Noll's death, his elegy,
Contain fine words of rare simplicity:

    "Valour, religion, friendship, prudence died
    "At once with him, and all that's good beside."

I'm a fan. You can tell. It's no surprise
That this perfect verse brings tears to the eyes.
There's more, much more. Forgive me if I quote.
Marvell's a wonder, a poet of note.

    "I saw him dead. A leaden slumber lies
    "And mortal sleep over those wakeful eyes.
    "Oh human glory vain, oh death, oh wings,
    "Oh worthless world, oh transitory things!"

Unless Marvell saw him on his deathbed –
Oliver the man, actually dead –
These verses are something of a fiction.
I'm loth to be the one to cause friction
In poetic circles, but the truth is
Cromwell's body caused a terrible tizz.
They botched the embalming procedure. Pooh!
The smell was quite horrid, I'm telling you.
His body was buried without delay
In Westminster Abbey where, to this day,
It should have lain at rest, unmolested.
Yet, though his allies strongly protested,

Rhyming History

He was dug up at the Restoration –
Such was the level of detestation –
Carted (along with Ireton and Bradshaw,
Both long dead too, you had better be sure)
To Tyburn, where the corpse was hanged. His head,
As if to prove he was properly dead,
Was hacked off and later spiked on a pole,
Where it stayed rotting for years. On the whole,
I think poor Noll deserved a kinder fate.

His skull did find its way, at any rate,
In recent years, back to his old college,
Sidney Sussex, Cambridge. To my knowledge,
Only a select few know its whereabouts,
To protect it from vandals and lager louts.

Marvell might have observed his effigy,
Lying in state for all the world to see,
At Somerset House, in great majesty.
As royally accoutred as could be,
Oliver had more the air of a King
In death (ironic) than ever living.
For three glorious weeks he lay in state –
His waxen image did, at any rate –
This in accordance with age-old practice.
Most dead Queens and Kings were decked out like this,
For public inspection. A royal crown
They placed on his head. Cromwell turned it down
In life. Dead, it appears he had no choice –
Hardly, I'd venture, a cause to rejoice.

Oliver's successor

Who next? His elder son. 'Tumbledown Dick',
So-called. Insulting nicknames tend to stick,
But the new Protector was far from thick.
Richard, in truth, didn't do too badly,
Given the hand that he'd been dealt. Sadly,

Cromwell and the Commonwealth

However, despite an adequate brain,
A strong sense of purpose and, in the main,
A worthy disposition, the sheer strain
Of his new office, its enormity,
Defeated him. He failed, not ignobly,
Rather with honour. Dismally prepared,
The more he tried, the more poor Dick despaired.
Where old Oliver had walked a tightrope
Between the factions, Richard couldn't cope.

In a nutshell, where the father was strong,
The son made it up as he went along.
He simply lacked the personality
For government. Oliver, quite frankly,
Was to blame. His modest, retiring son
Was a dreadful choice. The damage was done.

Yet the transfer of power was smooth. Why?
Opponents were keeping their powder dry.
Royalists were nervous. Restoration
Seemed a long way off. In truth, the nation
Was not missing the Stuarts overmuch.
The idea of monarchy, as such,
Was not unpopular – never had been.
But folk at large were rather less than keen
To hazard all that Cromwell had achieved.
Besides, if Clarendon's to be believed,
In his *History*, the King's condition
Was never more hopeless. The position,
By contrast, of the Protector was strong.
The Army, by all accounts, was 'on song';
Foreign governments expressed their delight
At Richard's 'accession'. Sweetness and light.

All governments enjoy a honeymoon.
Cromwell suffered a tumble all too soon.
The rival factions, already discussed,
Declared their hands, as he'd have known they must.

Rhyming History

The Army presented a petition.
Fleetwood (an aspiring politician)
Was proposed as new Commander-in-Chief,
Over the Protector (beyond belief) –
An early challenge to Richard's power.

George Monck

General Monck (stronger by the hour)
Proffered, from Scotland, this helpful advice:
Cromwell would pay a most terrible price
Were he to accept the role of Fleetwood
As Commander. It could come to no good.
In addition, Monck advised, Richard should
Call a Parliament without delay.

This Dick did. Less inspired, I have to say,
Was his appointment (to widespread dismay)
Of Fleetwood as Commander nonetheless,
But subordinate to him. I confess
To some confusion here. No surprise
That this unlikely, messy compromise
At very best was seen as temporary.
Cromwell was left uneasy, Fleetwood wary.

Monck emerged as a pivotal figure.
He'd served King Charles with spirit and vigour
In the first Civil War. He was captured,
Imprisoned and (so I've read) enraptured
(In prison) by one Mrs. Nan Radford,
His laundry lady. To level the score,
As it were, he fought in the first Dutch War,
Appointed, at the age of forty-four,
An Admiral by Cromwell. As we'll see,
George Monck's overarching philosophy
Was that soldiers should serve. The Army
Was for fighting wars. Ditto the Navy.
Interfere in politics? No, siree!

Cromwell and the Commonwealth

One useful trait, his taciturnity,
Served Monck bravely in the rudderless days
Following honest Dick's fall. Beyond praise
Was his clean grasp of a situation,
Incisive and clear. George saved the nation,
Paving the rough path to Restoration.

All that's for later. Monck's reputation
Was enhanced as Governor of Scotland,
Oliver's 'pro-consul'. His even hand,
Mature sense of purpose and level head
Brought peace (against the odds, it must be said)
To that unhappy and disordered land;
Which makes it easier to understand
Why Fleetwood and his cronies tried and tried
(But failed) to get the General on side.

Richard Cromwell's Parliament

Now, back to the plot. Where were we? Oh, yes –
Dick's new Parliament. I must confess,
Events weren't moving Richard's way at all.
The writing, sad to say, was on the wall.
When the new Parliament assembled,   **1659**
The sorry truth is it more resembled
A dog's breakfast than a legislature.
Some folk even questioned what it was for.
And what of its powers? No one was sure!

As for its membership: 'Commonwealthsmen',
Opposed to the Protector; some 'swordsmen',
So-called (few in number), for the Army;
Royalists (sycophantic and smarmy);
Presbyterians; and some of Dick's men
(Though not enough). It wasn't if, but when
This odd, unlikely edifice would collapse.
Could Cromwell work some magic? Well, perhaps.
He urged the members all to be good chaps
And labour for an early settlement
To further strong and stable government.

Army *versus* Parliament

Some hope! Members were only united –
A few, I'm told, got very excited –
On the hoary subject of Army power.

Relations became increasingly sour
As the Commons resolved to ride roughshod
Over Army demands. Soldiers, by God,
Had made the country what it was today!
Such burning issues as arrears of pay,
Indemnities for conduct in the past,
Freedom of association – this last,

In particular, a hard nut to crack –
Dominated debate. Dick lacked the knack
(Unlike his father) of divide and rule.
The young Protector was nobody's fool,
But he wouldn't face a problem head on.
He'd read a petition then pass it on
To Parliament, and his chance was gone.

The Commons voted, believe it or not –
I have to say, they deserved all they got –
That no meeting of officers should take place
Without Commons' agreement and (to save face)
The Lord Protector's too. A perfect disgrace.

Or was it? The Army needed curbing.
The officers' demands were disturbing,
Arrogant, high-handed – nay, insoluble.
Nor was Parliament indissoluble,
But it was loth to learn the lessons of the past.
In goading the military, it couldn't last.
Dick was stuck between a hard place and a rock.
As if he, not the Army, stood in the dock,
He meekly backed off. The 'grandees', so-called,
Had won hands down. The people were appalled.
Parliament was dissolved. No blood was shed,
The Protectorate, though? As good as dead.

Parliament dissolved

The rollercoaster ride towards Restoration
Was gathering pace. The sudden dissolution
Left something of a void. Lying through his back teeth,
Fleetwood wrote to Monck, insisting (beyond belief)
That Dick had dismissed the Commons as he thought fit.
The Army had simply nothing to do with it!
Don't imagine Monck believed a word, however.
Our friend kept his counsel. He was far too clever

Rhyming History

To declare his hand, still less fall in with Fleetwood.
He kept well out of it, as a good soldier should.

'Good soldier' isn't a term, in this context,
That I'd employ for John Lambert. Any pretext,
Any, would this vain man use to promote himself.
Side-lined by Oliver, he'd languished on the shelf,
Kicking his heels. But in Richard's Parliament
He'd made something of a comeback, giving full vent
To his naked distain for the Protectorate.
Yet his colleagues were suspicious, some dead set
Against him (Fleetwood, for one). Lambert's thrusting style
Was not to all tastes, proud-hearted and infantile.

Wary of Lambert, a number of the grandees
Were prepared to accept Dick, but stripped if you please,
Though Protector still, of all effective power
Over their precious Army! What a shower!
No one had the faintest notion what to do.
Divided and anxious, their options were few.

The Rump… again…

So they turned to the only body they knew,
The Rump! They recalled the Rump! Well, wouldn't you?
Probably not, if you'd any sense at all.
It certainly tickled William Lenthall,
Now approaching seventy. He, you'll recall,
Was Speaker of the Commons when the late King
Burst into the Chamber (not quite the done thing)
To demand where those Five Members were hiding.
William was back! The old Parliament
(The Rump, that is) returned yet again. This lent,
At best, a small vestige of authority
To the *régime*. The Army, quite patently,
Still ruled the roost. What of poor Tumbledown Dick?
Soldier on? Bow out? He could take his pick,

And he did. Graciously he left the stage.
A civilised man in a violent age,
He declined to be the cause of fresh bloodshed
By fighting to the last. Fine man. Enough said.

The 'new' Rump met in May. At first, it seemed,
It had a place. But while the Commons dreamed
Of better times ahead, the Army schemed.

Booth's uprising

In August a royalist uprising
Was suppressed. This was hardly surprising,
Given the dismal organisation
And low level of communication
Among Charles' supporters. Confirmation
Of their plight was had when Lambert, no less,
Routed Sir George Booth who, out to impress,

Rhyming History

Had rallied his troops at Chester. The Rump
Gave Lambert scant credit. That dreadful chump
Sir Arthur Haselrig, thorn in the side
Of Charles the First (though not a regicide),
And one who gave both Cromwells a rough ride,
Flirted with political suicide
By contriving to face down the Army
In the Commons. This was frankly barmy,
Given Lambert's comprehensive success
Against Sir George. Timing though, I confess,
Was not one of Sir Arthur's greater strengths.

It seems he'd go to almost any lengths
To insult the officers. Haselrig
Badly overplayed his hand. He talked big,
Purporting, he claimed, not to care a fig
For grievances such as arrears of pay,
And other 'sulks' that wouldn't go away.

Lambert seizes the initiative

Lambert was livid. It was showdown time.
Forget the fact he'd committed no crime,
The House of Commons ordered his arrest.
To no one's surprise, he rose to the test
And forcibly shut down Parliament!
At ease, it seems, and in his element,
He rallied his troops (his very own *coup*:
There was little even Fleetwood could do)
And refused to let any Rumpers through.
As he 'closed off' the Commons (in effect),
All hopes of accommodation were wrecked.

Monck was informed of events, as ever.
I did read that Lambert (boxing clever)
Made Fleetwood write the letter! What he said,
I've no notion. But Monck, I'll bet, saw red.

Still, though, he bided his time. George refused
To be drawn in. The Rump had been abused.
What right had officers to interfere
In government? Suffer Lambert? No fear.
'Lord' Lambert, he dubbed him, with irony.
Yet Monck felt sure, with utter certainty,
The time was nigh when, of necessity,
He'd be forced to act. His philosophy
Of non-intervention in politics
Would be sorely challenged. Pyrotechnics
Were quite simply not his style. Have no doubt.
He would watch while others burnt themselves out,
And so it proved. Messrs. Lambert, Fleetwood,
Desborough... Wicked or misunderstood?

Merely misguided, in my book at least.
Be that as it may. As tension increased,
Monck continued to keep his powder dry.
He declared for the Rump, but didn't try
(Wise move) to insinuate himself too soon
Into English affairs. Lambert's 'honeymoon'
Was short-lived. The Army was divided.
Although (oddly) it had been decided
To keep Fleetwood as Commander-in-Chief,
Lambert had his hands on the ropes. Good grief,
What a prospect! Protector? Dictator? King?
God forbid! Anything but that, anything!

Fleetwood's resignation

The military had its work cut out
Quelling riots in London. There's no doubt
(To my mind, anyway) that anarchy
Stalked the streets. The Committee of Safety,
So-called, was losing its grip. The Army
Loosened its stranglehold on Westminster
When Fleetwood, sensing something sinister

(Poor lamb), threw in the sponge (can you believe?)
And resigned his office on Christmas Eve!
The Rump was back. How many times was that?
I've forgotten just how often it sat.
Fewer than a dozen? I'll eat my hat.

Monck's aid was no longer necessary.
But the die was cast. Expressed quite simply,
The General was on his way. Fairfax
(Remember him?) pledged his support. "Relax!"
Monck assured the Rump, "I come in the cause
"Of freedom and peace." Cue, muted applause.
Many trusted Monck, but by no means all.
The royalist writing was on the wall.
George had fought for the late King. When he called
For 'free' elections, Rumpers were appalled.
They knew that they hadn't a hope in hell
Of being returned. And yes, time did tell.

Lambert's collapse

Monck arrived on February the 3rd –   **1660**
In the capital, that is. There was word
That he came 'for himself'. This was absurd.
John Lambert's forces had dwindled away
In the face of Monck's. John collapsed that day.
Fleetwood had quit the field, to which I say,
Good riddance. He lacked fibre, anyway.
And Desborough? Does anybody care?
He made no mark, as far as I'm aware.

Monck's progress

Which left Monck… "Nature abhors a vacuum",
So we're told. The elephant in the room,
Of course, was Charles Stuart: Charles the Second.
In hindsight it's generally reckoned

Cromwell and the Commonwealth

That Monck was hell-bent on Restoration
From the start. Frankly, that's speculation.
We can't be certain. This much we do know:
He was sure by now the Rump had to go.
Haselrig, recalcitrant so-and-so,
Irritated Monck to such a degree
That had he not determined already
To disband the Rump he would, probably,
Have done so on the first occasion
If only out of sheer frustration!

Old members of the Long Parliament
(Remember them?), in all the excitement,
Resumed their seats, thereby 'ousting' the Rump.
Haselrig and his cronies got the hump,
But no one cared. Reform was on its way.
Pride's Purge belonged to quite another day.

George Monck was still giving nothing away.
He played a blinder, I'm happy to say.
The will of Parliament he'd obey.
Who was he, a mere servant, to gainsay
Its acts, its dictates and its great decrees?
After almost two decades, if you please,
The Long Parliament ended its life
By its own hand. Speculation was rife.

Who would succeed in the new elections?
Returns exceeded all expectations.
The Rumpers were trounced, Republicans too;
Presbyterians fared poorly: a few
Were elected, though in truth not a lot.
The old guard fully deserved what they got.
Haselrig was out. That raised quite a cheer
In royalist circles, from what I hear.
Those sympathetic to the royal cause
Were returned in droves. It was time to pause,

Rhyming History

To take stock: eighteen years of Civil War,
Regicide, Commonwealth, Cromwell and more.

Yet all this changed in the blink of an eye.
How did it happen, you're asking – and why?

No one, in truth, was especially keen
On the House of Stuart but, as we've seen,
The country was low on alternatives!
The rebels gave way to conservatives.
George Monck, who had been for Charles all along,
Led from the front. The General was strong,
Determined and (thank Heaven) practical.
His campaign from the start was tactical,
Discreet and not devoid of mystery.
In one of the great *coups* of history,
He prepared the ground for the King's return,
Displaying *panache* at every turn.

Kings, Lords and Commons

The new Parliament (or 'Convention',
Since not summoned, I feel bound to mention,
By the Crown) resolved, with indecent haste –
As if to show there was no time to waste –
That government should henceforth be by King,
Lords and Commons. The pace was breathtaking.

The General was in daily contact
With the Monarch, advising him with tact
(And some caution). One unfortunate fact
Was that Charles, in exile, was still living
In the Spanish Netherlands. Forgiving
As his loyal subjects at home might be,
This (as far as the General could see)
Was a terrible start. A guest of Spain?
Hardly the best of beginnings. Insane.

Cromwell and the Commonwealth

The Declaration of Breda

Move, Monck recommended, to Breda (Dutch)
And woo the people from there. George's touch,
Surefooted and sound, contributed much
To the unexpectedly peaceful path
To Restoration. One's temped to laugh,
It seemed too easy. Charles' 'Declaration
Of Breda', so-called, assured the nation
Of his good faith. His father's enemies
Were offered pardons and indemnities –
Regicides excepted (the Convention
To decide precisely whom). Attention,
Too, was given to the burning question
Of a land settlement, a suggestion
Generally welcomed by those whose estates
Had been sold or sequestered. Now, what placates
One faction can often upset another.
The Civil Wars set brother against brother
And, in like manner, this alleged 'settlement'
Gave rise to many a bitter argument.

All that's for later. Charles (no angel he)
Could act with shabbiness – nay, perfidy.
His declared preference for liberty
To tender consciences, however,
Was a masterstroke. Subtle and clever.

Charles made all the right noises. Edward Hyde,
With Monck in tandem, urged him to decide.
Those who wished to lay down limitations
On royal authority, 'privations'
Akin to those they had sought to impose
On Charles the First, were brushed aside. Monck chose
To go the whole hog and George Monck, God knows,
Held the cards. When occasion arose
He would seize the moment. Seize it he did.
Should any man oppose him, God forbid!

The return of King Charles

And so it was that at the end of May
Charles made ready. The King was on his way.
On the 29th (the royal birthday)
He rode into London. The bells rang out.
Some 20,000 men (or thereabout)
Attended their sovereign. Fountains flowed
With wine, all the day long. Lining the road,
In their finest array, the people cheered,
As their long-awaited monarch appeared.

The famous diarist, John Evelyn, wrote
(His words are perfect, it's best if I quote):
"I stood in the Strand" (an eye-witness, you see)
"And beheld it and blessed God" (then, touchingly)
"And all this without one drop of blood". Rarely,
If ever, can a moment in history
Have been captured with such sensitivity.

So began what's generally reckoned
The dissolute reign of Charles the Second.
The King's considered a perfect disgrace –
By some. Not by me. Kindly watch this space.

Bibliography

Maurice Ashley, *England in the Seventeenth Century* (Penguin, 3rd ed. 1961)

John Aubrey, *Brief Lives*, ed. Oliver Lawson Dick (Secker & Warburg, 1949)

Martyn Bennett, *Oliver Cromwell* (Routledge, 2006)

Martyn Bennett, *The English Civil War* (Longman, 1995)

Charles Carlton, *Charles I, the Personal Monarch* (Routledge, 2nd ed. 1995)

Barry Coward, *The Stuart Age. England 1603-1714* (Pearson Education, 3rd ed. 2003)

Christopher Durston, *Charles I* (Routledge, 1998)

Encyclopaedia Britannica (2010)

Antonia Fraser, *Cromwell, Our Chief of Men* (Phoenix, 2002)

Peter Gaunt, *Oliver Cromwell* (Blackwell, 1996)

Charles George, *The Stuarts. A Century of Experiment, 1603-1714* (Hart-Davis Educational, 1975)

C. P. Hill, *Who's Who in Stuart Britain* (Shepheard-Walwyn, 1988)

S. J. Houston, *James I* (Longman, 2nd ed. 1995)

John Miller, *The Stuarts* (Hambledon, 2006)

John Morrill, *The Stuarts* (in *The Oxford History of Britain*, ed. Kenneth O. Morgan – Oxford University Press, 2001)

Ivan Roots, *The Great Rebellion* (The History Press, 2009)

G. M. Trevelyan, *A Shortened History of England*
(Penguin, 1959)

John Wroughton, *The Stuart Age, 1603-1714*
(Longman, 1997)